Counseling and Creativity

Reflections

Counseling and Creativity

Reflections

George Cambell Hage, Ed. D., Ph.D.

One Spirit Press
Portland, Oregon

Copyright © 2015 by George Cambell Hage

Arbitary Sense of Self Copyright © 2015 by Corey Smith

No part of this publication may be reproduced, stored in a retrieval system, or transmitted in any form or by any means, electronic, mechanical, photocopying, recording, scanning, or otherwise, except as permitted under Section 107 or 108 of the 1976 United States Copyright Act, without either the prior written permission of the author, or authorization through payment of the appropriate per-copy fee to the Copyright Clearance Center, 222 Rosewood Drive, Danvers, MA 01923, (978) 750-8400, fax 978-646-8600 or on the web at www.copyright.com.

LCCN: 2015907557

ISBN: 978-1-893075-57-3

Library of Congress Cataloging-in-Publication Data

George Hage 2015.

Counseling and Creativity, Reflections George Cambell Hage Includes bibliographical references and index.

1. Psychology—Counseling 2. Sociology—Relationship with poverty and underserved. 3. Philosophy—Ontology; self dtermination. 5. Arts. 6 .Cultural Diversity

One Spirit Press
Portland, Oregon
www.onespiritpress.com

Dedication

I am remembering all who have contributed to my formation as a counselor and therapist: Teachers, Professors, Clinical Supervisors, Consultants, Trainers, Colleagues and Support Personnel and all of the Counseling and Social Services Agencies over the past twenty-five years of my counseling experience.

I am remembering and acknowledging Insight Human Services including Supervisors, Clinical Supervisors, Colleagues, and Support Staff for their encouragement, training and support over the past ten years as this agency has contributed much to my formation as a counselor and that, in turn, has given rise to the counseling and client experiences that are demonstrated in this book

Contents

Chapter One
An Ontological Approach — 3

Chapter Two
Curative Awareness — 27

Chapter Three
Infinite Possibilities — 39

Chapter Four
Contemporary Personality Theory — 65

Chapter Five
Three Personality Sketches — 71

Chapter Six
Cultural and Artistic
Approaches to Counseling — 89

Chapter Seven
Counseling and Personality Portraiture — 105

Chapter Eight
Assumptions and Conclusion — 123

Notes — 131
Bibliography — 142
Index — 151
About The Author — 164

Note to Reader

This study focuses on the artistic, ethnic, and academic dimensions of personality that become paradigms for creative counseling. It shows how defining and assessing multicultural client personalities was accomplished. The resultant ends are works of art through the counselor as artist and mentor, thereby, working to transform multicultural client personalities into artists who, in turn, compose unique self-portraits of wholeness and self-actualization.

One

An Ontological Approach

Self-Awareness

Why am I a counselor? What purpose do I find in Counseling? What am I achieving as a counselor? These three questions are approached through my autobiography with the techniques of counselor self-reflection and multicultural counseling. Self-reflection involves looking at the personality and considering attitudes, values, thoughts and behaviors in the course of professional life. This also involves cultural life and experiences and how these play into relating with culturally diverse clients.[1] With self-reflection, the interrelationship of professional self is being treated and correlated with the artistic nature of counseling approaches and the nature of multicultural clientele as works of art.

This results in a heightened awareness of self and psyche, namely, self-awareness. In essence, the self-reflecting one interacts with psyche and self. Psyche refers to one's being, and self refers to one's identity as person, persona, or personality. The self enters into the darkness of one's being and converses with it. Also such conversing involves listening to one's being as it will speak back to self. Such engagement of the psyche, through past, present and future, results in the apprehension of the unity of self and psyche.

To *apprehend* in the Greek means to *grab onto*, as in fully comprehending, namely, a comprehension not merely in terms of mind, but also in terms of heart. In such *apprehension*, self enters into the antithesis of heart and mind, and in the process of its dialogue with psyche, self synergizes the heart/mind antithesis. Thought no longer remains only cognition or affects remain solely emotions. Rather thoughts and emotions synergize as living emotive-thoughts. Thoughts and emotions conjoin as a unity engendering understanding and knowing that is above mundane understanding and knowing.

That is, understanding and knowing become *wisdom*. *Wisdom* emerges from the inclusive psyche and self as one whole being. Such a being is totally self-aware in that self and psyche complete one another as a whole, for the unity of the whole is energized in the unity of heart and mind. Thoughts no longer run randomly apart from emotions and emotions no long run randomly apart from thoughts. The same may be said of the physical and metaphysical. Rather they complement one another as living wholes.

Inter-reflectively, such as self-awareness involves the awareness of self and psyche as complementing one another while entering into the *apprehension* of world and being beyond self and psyche. Such being and world, although perceived as outside of self and psyche, no longer remain as antithetical to self and psyche. Rather being and world become complements of self and psyche. For in one's dialogue of self and psyche in darkness one enters into light.

Also, the inter-reflective interaction of self with psyche, while moving from darkness to light, moves from darkness to light with and in being and world. And, as said, this inter-reflective interaction is centered in the heart and mind moving from the darkness that divides them into the light that synergizes them. In turn, such synergy complements human person and being with all things comprising world and being beyond.

Socrates once taught: "the unexamined life is not worth living." One must enter into self and psyche critically and analytically. Likewise Jesus taught that we must judge self before judging others, that we must consider the beam in our own eye before considering the speck in the other's eye. Socrates, being Greek, considered living in terms of mind and intellect. Jesus, being Hebrew, taught in terms of the heart as intellect. As he once taught: "Out of the heart proceeds every evil thought and imagination." Jesus also taught; "If a man even looks upon a woman to negatively desire or 'lust' after her, he hath already committed adultery in his heart." The heart is the center of psyche and self. In Eastern Orthodox thought, heart and mind are separate through the fall of Adam. Hence, one has mastered self when heart becomes the seat of mind instead of these remaining fragmented oppositions. Essentially, Socrates and Jesus taught the same thing but took a different symbolic approach as defined by Greek and Hebrew cultural traditions.

Thus living begins and ends with this dialogue of self with psyche and both of them dialogue with the world as other. This synergistic unity of human being with other engenders Jung's *individuation*, Maslow's *self-actualization* and Roger's *becoming* a fully integrated person. This is the very heart of creativity and spirituality. This is the *transformed* human being who lives *transforming* the world. This is the end of living, counseling and teaching. This is *wisdom*, the life of the congruent *whole*. This is the end of philosophy, science and art and is the beginning of wholeness of self, personality and psyche.

In this study, this dialogue emerges and ends with the counselor and client resulting in self and other as *works of art*. The *work of art* displays the *congruency* of *beauty* with reason, logic and proportion, the congruency of heart with mind, self and other, psyche and world, seen and unseen, the physical and metaphysical, valuing and ordering, darkness and light, and the like. In such a human being, the final *transformation* of self, psyche and other as world begins as the *alpha* in the human soul, the depths of psyche and self, and through past, present and future action moves to the *omega*, the *telos* of human being and other. This is the *creative action* of *wisdom*, beauty and wholeness.

My awareness of self as counselor is due to

considering related experiences in the field since 1989. Through applying these experiences in conjunction with counseling theory, a definition and theory of creative counseling is being formulated while applying paradigms of music and the fine arts.

In 1989, I entered counseling in the capacities of teacher, minister and philosopher being well educated and trained in music, art, psychological learning theory and philosophies of learning. During the process of counseling, I became licensed as a professional counselor in 1995 when the North Carolina Board of Licensed Professional Counselors came into existence. Over the years, my formation as a professional counselor has been fostered by well experienced, educated clinical supervisors, educators and colleagues of the varied therapeutic disciplines.

I hold doctorates in education and theology. The former is a Doctor of Education in Curriculum and Teaching, Grades K-12, while the latter is a Doctor of Philosophy in Eastern Orthodox Studies. Aside from 25 years of counseling experience, I have acquired experience through teaching at the high school and community college levels. My pastoral experience has included church leadership with youth, adults and seniors in a small mainline Protestant denomination. Within the last two years, my ministry continues in the Eastern Orthodox context, the church of my grandparents.

In graduate school, I studied psychological anthropology, called personality and culture. In these studies, the psychodynamics of values acquisition and the formation of self and personality were emphasized. These educational and philosophical studies not only involved theories and approaches to learning (the epistemological dimension of philosophy) but also the dimension of values (the axiological dimension of philosophy). Also, through anthropology, philosophy and theology, values formation was related to learning and cultural being (the ontological dimension of philosophy). As a counseling professional, my approach to clientele includes culturally contextual personalities being shaped by the dynamics of self within environment.

The experiences of other cultures and spiritualities have been considered in my writing. Such experiences include not only growing up in an ethnic home but serving as a counselor, teacher, Protestant minister and later an Eastern Orthodox priest. These cultures range geographically from the areas of the Middle East, the Greek and Slavic nations of Russia and Eastern Europe to the African nations and even Western Europe, Latin America, and the cultural diversity of the United States and Canada. At the same time, I experienced the unique opportunity of studying theology in an Eastern Orthodox Seminary as a young man. There I became exposed to cultural diversity through students and faculty comprising nationals from the above regions and countries.

While looking over the years of autobiographical and counseling experiences, the perimeters of this self-study include my current treatment agency of professional counseling over the past ten years. My service has taken place in the mental health division of this drug and alcohol community agency. I have provided counseling and therapy for youth and their families in the areas of drug and alcohol prevention, mental health, and education. These clients are culturally diverse. My service as counselor has involved youth of Anglo-American heritage and those of western European heritage. Also, counseling included those of many first-and second-generation Latino cultures and, of course, many of African-American heritages.

My ministry has pastored many, including children and youth, middle aged and senior aged individuals and many families. In teaching, I have interacted with many of all ages (from kindergarten through senior citizen ages) both individually and in groups. In counseling, I have engaged with youth as individuals and in the contexts of groups and families. Youth age ranges have been approximately 12 through 25 years. These clients have been referred principally by families and friends, courts, schools, hospitals, physicians' offices, social services and other counseling and mental health agencies.

Experiences of cultural diversity began in my home growing up. Being of first-and second-generation Lebanese stock, living in Huntington, West Virginia, my parents were third cousins whose parents had immigrated to the United States from Kfeir, Lebanon. This village is located 900 miles above sea level in the mountains of South East Lebanon.[2] My parents were of Greek Orthodox heritage under the ancient Patriarchate of Antioch in Damascus, Syria. However, in our formative years, my siblings and I were reared in the Episcopal Church due to the unavailability of an Eastern Orthodox Church in our hometown.

I was the eldest of seven children, three boys and four girls. Growing up, I was exposed the heritage of Lebanese relatives gathering together and speaking Arabic. They and my mother often cooked Lebanese meals. At the same time, mother and dad befriended many among Greek, Italian and Jewish immigrants. In my later adolescent years, we spent much time in the Greek Orthodox Church where my younger brother served as altar boy, and the priest was teaching me the Byzantine chant of the Divine Liturgy. I had also spent a couple of years chanting and playing the organ for a local Roman Catholic Church. I became exposed to cultural diversities through both Latin and Greek liturgies.

Mother and dad were artistically inclined and college educated. Dad completed three years of college majoring in political science, and mother completed two years majoring in business. Both parents sang, with dad being a lyric tenor and mother being a mezzosoprano. They encouraged us to study music and art. Mother was talented in art as was her mother.

Mother and dad initiated my study of piano at eight years of age, and by the eighth grade, my interest in piano performance and music composition was ignited through listening to Beethoven's Moonlight Sonata in music appreciation class. Enthrallment of the sonata's beauty drove me to increase piano practice from approximately two through eight hours daily. Eventually, with the advice of a violin and theory professor from the local university, my parents paid for advanced music lessons with a piano professor at that same university. I began giving full recitals in high school. Then in college, I mastered the piano technic of Madame and Leon Conus.[3]

Although I graduated with a bachelor's degree in music, education and performance, I continued studying art through and after college. I had drawn and painted since early childhood. In fact, I engaged in art before I spoke, not actually talking until five years of age. In fact, I would strive to sign with my hands as well as by drawing and painting. Mother drew and painted with me while teaching me to speak.

Through kindergarten and the first grade, mother facilitated my reading and comprehension skills, yet the later remained weak until my freshman year in college. I remained fundamentally nonverbal but demonstrated a strong symbolic orientation through the arts. While in elementary school, mother also strove to enhance my verbal ability through speech and drama lessons. She had contracted with a local speech educator whose husband taught at the university. Through this lady, I was engaged in many drama and poetry lessons and recitals.

Through experiences in counseling, learning and education, I became very conscious of the symbolic in language, in the arts and in the speaking and behavior of clients. I have realized my clients as creative beings striving for meaning in their lives. Therefore, my call as counselor is to facilitate this.

Having studied teaching and curriculum, I developed a philosophy of education based upon the creative processes of the artist. I see both counseling and teaching as helping clients to become artists through creating compositions on manuscripts and canvases of their lives. This approach leads clients to realize and create self-portraiture of balance and wholeness. Clients learn positive self-direction and self-management as artists who freely design and create compositions demonstrating the beauty of wholeness and balance.

In fact, such beauty denotes the end of art and composition. Counselees are empowered to consciously engage in choices that are transformative. This most often goes against the grain of counselees [in place of counseling] often taught in school to engage in limited choices that are "black" or "white," "yes" or "no," and "right" or "wrong." They most likely never become encouraged to look into themselves and cultivate self-analytic skills. Resultantly, they most likely lack the ability to relate to the *how*, *where* and *what* of their academic exposures in school. Clients are discouraged from looking into themselves as whole persons and valuing themselves as truly purposeful beings with unique, creative and purposeful places in the schema of being. I have observed many clients as oppressed and alienated in the school culture.

In addition, many clients are reared in home environments with no father figure and a weak mother figure. In family therapy, many families are observed as dysfunctional. These families most likely are not displaying the balance of many two-parent families with middle to upper middle incomes.

Two-parent families tend to earn middle to upper middle class incomes whether Hispanic, African-American or Anglo-American, and single-parent families of all ethnicities usually earn lower class incomes. In addition, clients from two-parent families demonstrate more success in school and counseling. Conversely, clients from single-parent families tend to be not as successful. Although I experienced exceptions to the "rules" stated, I also have emphasized these exceptions.

Overall, through spiritual and multicultural counseling, emphasis is placed on the socio-cultural contexts of counselees. Serving approximately 100 to 400 of these clients per school year, I experience their sociocultural situations. These situations are defined by economic and family structures including ethnicity, religion, and family size.

My background indicates commonality with Hispanic clientele and their families. Like my grandparents and relatives, first generation parents of Hispanic clients are living in poverty while trying to attain citizenship, thereby leaving these clients caught in the middle of these struggles. Either one or both parents are working and are looking to relatives for assisting in the care of counselees and their siblings. Unlike many of the parents of Hispanic counselees, my parents were fluent in English. Their parents learned English by struggling with it as did my grandparents. Often I heard my relatives and parents converse in Arabic and "broken" English.

Mother and dad were self-employed restaurant proprietors while other relatives worked for others at whatever job they could find. My parents were college educated but worked to put themselves through school. Mother paid for her voice and piano lessons. She and dad claimed that in childhood, their parents were too poor to pay for such opportunities. Both parents began working while in high school. Likewise many Hispanic families and clients find themselves in a similar situation.

Many among Hispanic families are not receiving public assistance most likely due to not attaining citizenship and must continue to strive for this. They are looking to relatives, often living and working together with them for survival. Oftentimes, in two-parent Hispanic households, the father is working two and three jobs while the mother stays at home with the children. Hispanic families usually will include 2 or more children.

Similarly, many African-American clients and parents are living in poverty. Unlike many Hispanic families, they are able to receive public assistance. In African-American households, generally, one parent, most likely the mother or grandmother rears the children. Many are on public assistance, but exceptions to this observation most likely include single parents with employment. Nevertheless, clients of African-American and Hispanic families often find themselves at home alone when not in school. They usually "hang out" in the neighborhood with peers, who most likely include friends, siblings and cousins.

As a child growing up in school, especially in elementary and junior high school, I remember being looked askance by others among teachers and classmates. My awareness became heightened to consistently being treated differently yet not knowing why. I recall my sister, next to my age, being taunted. She displayed a dark olive complexion with long, dark-brown hair that my mother often curled each evening. Growing older, I became aware of my lack of resemblance to classmates. My physical features and olive complexion demonstrated characteristics of Middle Eastern lineage.

Upon entering high school, I performed on the piano very well. At the same time, due to where I lived, this glaring characteristic of my personality provoked laughter and even maltreatment from my peers, and at the restaurant, some customers were aloof to my parents. However, they ate and paid for meals while claiming they tasted really great and were a bargain.

This has helped me to empathize with Hispanic children and families as well as many African-American clients. They have three things going against them, namely, ethnicity, race and poverty. In school, they feel unwelcomed and often report being treated unfairly. They feel teachers and staff eyeing them as troublemakers. As I felt lost and rejected at school, so they are feeling this as well. With many Hispanic and African-American counselees, a deep fear and anxiety of school haunts them. They are troubled, often with depression and anxiety, due to the hollowness of feeling lost and rejected at school.

Due to ethnic race and poverty, these counselees most likely have to work harder than their Caucasian counterparts to achieve the same high grades. However, many give up due to believing they have no chance. Many Hispanic boys will look to their working fathers and elder working relatives as their rationale for quitting school in order to work. Some African-American clients also quit school in order to work. Nevertheless, many have no male role models at home. In contrast, many African-American males will engage in school sports and excel, especially, in basketball. African-American boys often look to one another for support due to absences of male role models at home.

My realization over the years is that I also have worked harder than many Anglo-American counterparts in school and in the employment setting. Through hard work alone and having a strong education, I have discovered not receiving the rewards of success of many Anglo-American counterparts. Of course, as an Arab-American, Affirmative Action is legally inaccessible, but I also experience from the Anglo-American cultural system, the dominant system, not being included among Anglo-Americans. Like African-Americans and Hispanic Americans, I have been victimized through much prejudicial stereotyping.

Nevertheless, I have learned to accept myself and have developed pride in my heritage, talents, education and work. Since the lower grades of school, I continued working to earn high grades and mastering the piano despite the critical downplays received from many classmates and some teachers. As suggested earlier, growing up in school was an unhappy experience, but I empathize with clients encouraging them to self-reflect, to *lay hold on*[4] their talents and to find pride in themselves, their heritage and their work as students. I am hurt when clients give up, quit school, and lack positive self-respect. Therefore, I offer clients extended efforts of genuineness, belongingness and unconditional positive regard.[5]

Worldview[6] and Personality

The purpose of most counselors is to lead clients into wholeness, as fully developing and blossoming personalities empowered to find success in life. The art of counseling facilitates clients toward wholeness and self-actualization through treating their needs and issues.[7] Due to the uniqueness of clients, counseling approaches include the multicultural and eclectic. Currently, my counseling approaches include the evidenced based practices of cognitive behavior therapy and motivational enhancement therapy. At the same time, I apply person-centered, Logotherapy, Rogerian and other humanistic therapies while involving counselees in art and writing. In striving to reach the whole person, hopefully clients are guided to recreate their worldviews. Most clients often present with a fractured sense of world demonstrating many issues including thought disorders, illogical thinking and negative self-talk.

Our worldviews are reflected in our personality, and plays out in/as our consciousness. This axiom is derived through studying psychological anthropology and through experiences of family, culture, and schooling. Overall, this deduction results from negative and positive interactions with others among clients, parents, siblings, relatives, friends, strangers, teachers and fellow students. A counselor's enhanced consciousness of client worldviews is fundamentally derived from self-observation, which plays out as awareness of ego-self and personality.

A counselor must delve into anthropological studies of tribal, cultural worldviews. The consciousness of an individual's worldviews form the heart of linguistic structure and culture. Through the study of key metaphors, symbols, words and phrases in language, many traits of the human personality are exposited. We behave, dress and talk in ways that mark their culture and the uniqueness of their personalities. Anthropologists note that the heart of cultural worldviews is substantiated by the religious and spiritual foundation of cultures and tribal societies.

Through studying religion, philosophy, history, theology and anthropology, I cultivated a strong awareness of and sensitivity to the spirit of religion as the heart and life of respective cultures. Hence, Hispanic American, African-American and Anglo-

American have a strong cultural knowledge base. This, in turn, is seen through their personalities, generations of behavior and tradition, but much of this knowledge base remains unconscious to them. Through counseling and education, they increase consciousness of self and personality while moving through thoughts, emotions and behaviors defining their identities[8] as cultural beings.

In summary, I have presented self, through my story, thereby, defining personality in terms of worldview. Worldview suggests that I am one of generations of Arab-Lebanese males born in Huntington, West Virginia, a third descendent from the Lebanese village of Kfeir. The religion of Kfeir, being Greek Orthodox and Muslim, was transmitted through my parents and grandparents.

I was reared hearing and somewhat speaking the Arabic language, not totally conscious of the language. Mother and dad had insisted our learning English over and against Arabic with the belief that we must be American. My self and personality became acculturated with the conflict of Arab-Lebanese and Anglo-American values and aspirations. At the same time, this conflict continued due to the stereotyping and prejudice of fellow students, some school staff and others.

I found myself overwhelmed with feelings of inferiority. Conversely, these feelings ignited within my being the drive toward high achievement. Today, my consciousness is filled with the belief and value that acculturation energizes conflict between third world Arab and first world Anglo-American. Within my personality, feelings of inferiority meant being defeated while striving for high achievement meant being successful. This led to a discovery of concepts underpinning defeat and success as being tied to long strings of synonyms in opposition to one another within the American English language and culture.

Being Eastern Orthodox by faith and culture, I looked for fulfillment in Protestantism, but with dissatisfaction, I returned to Orthodoxy. Through Bible College and in the pastorate, I experienced feelings of displacement. Through my parents and grandparents, I was enculturated into Arab-Greek Orthodox Christianity, which also became my anchor in the strong value of humility over pride and arrogance. From this, my struggles impelled the acceptance of what I believed was the pride and arrogance of success. Instead, I struggled with the tension of seeking humility in success over pride in success.

Maturity and experience have empowered my grasp of becoming successful while striving for humility. Key metaphors of my worldview have been related to music, art, Greek, Balkan, and Middle Eastern cultures including the Greek Orthodox Church. Specifically, I have been motivated by key metaphors of saint, philosopher and wise man. These key metaphors actually reflect wholeness with balance, self-actualization, individuation, becoming and holiness.

Conversely, the key fragment implicitly influencing my worldview was that of the father image and my relationship to it. I was impelled with struggling to please my father while believing I was pleasing myself. This issue lay in my love of music. I really was diligent in piano practice often envisioning myself as a concert pianist. Piano became my key metaphor and the composer my secondary key metaphor.

Interestingly, I became open to the reality of my father's desire to become a concert musician. He was musically gifted pianistically and vocally. Instead he became a successful businessman and restaurant proprietor. Nevertheless, he always encouraged my diligence at the piano and in school. Upon arriving home from work nightly, he requested my playing music assigned by my piano instructor. In fact, during high school and early college years, this musical relationship with dad was very positive. Sadly, this bond was broken upon my decision to study for ministry and priesthood. In fact, our relationship became totally fragmented upon my choice to marry the lady whom I met in Bible College. She was majoring in religious education and was planning to become a missionary.

Upon entering my forties, I experienced emotional distress relating to the change of life and my paternal bond. Through my family physician, I was referred for counseling and therapy with a psychiatric resident at first and later continued therapy with his supervisor. During our interactions, we concluded that I most likely was confusing God with the shadow[9] of my father as the bitterness of rejection felt from dad was negatively impacting my spiritual life.

Importantly, in the Eastern Orthodox Greek and Arab worlds, God is the father figure. I was plagued with vivid dreams and nightmares. God and dad had become the other key metaphors of my worldview. Nevertheless, I was troubled with this therapeutic hypothesis, but eventually, my realization was awakened to the reality that while trying to please God I was actually trying to please my father. Dad was still empowering my life as he had implicitly wielded much influence in my high school and early college years.

Perhaps turning away from music became my way of turning away from dad. This may have been defined in my worldview unconsciously but was certainly conveyed indirectly by my father. Yet, in order to mend fragmentation and pain, I went forward with my life seeking to excel in philosophy and religion. In time, counseling became the way of synthesizing my diverse education as teacher, minister, musician and philosopher. Also, I have striven for success in marriage, which I have attained.

My worldview suggests the importance of Spirit and religion in my personality and life as bequeathed to me through Arabic Greek Orthodoxy. In Kfeir, my ancestors and relatives would gather around the Church as it was the center of family and community life. The Church was the center of the Eucharist depicting and conveying the very presence of Christ and the Holy Trinity. All other sacraments were celebrated around the Eucharist. Even secular occasions and festivals were held around the Eucharist. In essence, the Eucharist empowers all sacramental and secular life with the presence of Christ and in Him, God the Father and the Holy Spirit. Although my parents were not consistently involved in liturgical worship, the Spirit of the Church and Christ lived in their beliefs, attitudes and values. Of course, these were conveyed to our immediate family in terms of virtue, sacrifice, commitment and hard work.

In our family, the metaphor of Father, Son, and Holy Spirit, one God, worked itself out creating a personality of faith and God-centeredness in the Arabic-Greek Orthodox sense. We remember our great aunt telling stories of faith in Kfeir that she experienced as a young girl. The following story is unforgetful. She would say:

> A blind man named [Fouad] lived in our village. He begged daily and would also pray at the village Church daily. One day, while praying, [Fouad] heard a gentle female voice   say to him, [Fouad], you will from this day forth remain a blind man, but you shall be as one who sees. The person behind the female voice allowed the blind man to see her full of Light. He described her as the All-Holy One, the Blessed and Glorious Lady Theotokos and Ever Virgin Mary. From that day forward, Fouad moved about and lived in the village still blind but as one who sees.

From my Aunt's story, we learned of miracles being commonplace in Kfeir. We came to believe in and look for the good that is seemingly impossible daily.

In this light, I often think of the Cherokees who see in the center of their world the One whom they call the Great Spirit. They see this Great Spirit always working, healing and providing in their respective villages, and, at the same time, this same Spirit is moving in vegetable, animal and mineral. Native Americans see elements and living things of nature as being essential to their world. Hence, they consider animals as key metaphors depicting the Great Spirit living through their personalities and lives.[10] .

Likewise, Eastern Orthodox highly value vegetable, animal and mineral and their place in the Arabic and Greek and in the western European and Anglo-American worlds. All things have been redeemed, transfigured and glorified by Christ, the Resurrected One. Christ, the transcendent yet immanent One, fills and embraces all that is, namely, human, animal, vegetable and mineral. In the redemption of humankind, He transfigures and resurrects all of creation. Thus the Saints of Holy Orthodoxy embracing animals and nature are commonplace. The Saints depict our becoming transfigured in the glory of Christ. Also, in that transfiguration, the all of creation is glorified and human and animal again commune with another.

Overall, transfiguration and transformation depict the *terminus* of creation.[11] Through struggles, encounters and education, creative transformation becomes the end of helping, teaching, nurturing and loving others along with the creation. This is the essence of creative endeavor. The self of my worldview is the caregiver of being in conformity with nature while transfiguring the fallen in it. Reaching out to the fragmented, destitute, and alienated is transformative to man and nature, in that when one person is made whole, all living and nonliving through that person are healed and transfigured. When one person finds wholeness, they find unity with self and the circle of all life.

Effective counseling results in the transformation of clients as whole and creative personalities. However, transformation begins with counselor self-awareness and self-reflection. As Jesus teaches, one must see the speck in the eye of self before being empowered to see the beam in the eye of the other.[12] Counselors must become aware of the flow of thought and emotions through mind and heart. They must remain continually vigilant and mindful[13] of self. Counselors must respect and show empathy for others, as they desire the same to be shown them.

Counselors endeavor to live in harmony and connectedness with being. They demonstrate wholeness, healing and harmony to others that they may see these in the image of self and personality. In turn, others find encouragement toward empowerment and motivation, thereby, making necessary decisions of change that lead toward wholeness. Counselors, through example and methodology, see clients as unique personalities empowered to become unique compositions full of beauty. As all plants, animals, minerals and humans differ and by nature are fully unique so counselors facilitate uniqueness and wholeness in human clients.

Two

Curative Awareness

Counselor and Clients

I have been employed as an adolescent counselor for ten years in a substance abuse agency that also serves mental health clients. Youth are referred with substance abuse and/or mental health issues and needs. In assessing for treatment, data from clients and parents are gathered formulating a treatment plan based upon individual, family, educational, and treatment histories. In this agency, I am counseling with other clinicians: a licensed marital and family therapist, two clinical psychologists, one on the doctoral level and the other on the master's level and a psychiatrist.

Over the years, I have worked with both males and females. However, the vast majority of clients have included the male gender. Counseling in this agency as well as past ones involved referring female and male clients to counselors of their respective genders. Most often, such referrals reflected the sensitivity of gender related to treatment needs requiring commonality with gender related therapists. This way, effective treatment would most likely be assured.

In previous treatment agencies, I counseled individuals and families in the areas of residential care, foster care, and adoptions. I developed a strong sense of individual and family therapies as being contextual. Relatively, as with studying a philosophical treatise or even the Bible, I learned that in interpretation that word or phrase is never removed out of its written context. In scripture, for example, one does not evoke a thorough meaning of the word *love* until that word is traced through the books of the Bible and the treatises and paragraphs surrounding it. Then that word is compared to meanings of *love* in languages and cultures surrounding the books and treatises of scripture.

Likewise I have considered clients as living epistles, namely, as personalities understood and interpreted in their living and verbal context. Of course, the contexts of clients center on and begin with their immediate families, relatives and cultural contexts. In turn, cultural contexts are seen as transgenerational reaching to clients' nations of origins. Also, of importance to contextual therapy include clients' circle of friends, significant acquaintances, organizations and agencies within the greater community.[1]

For example, Hispanic clients may easily be traced to Latin American nations and culture. One may consider the following illustration and approach: Hispanic American Type X is a male or female, of 15 years, whose parents migrated to California from Mexico. This client most likely was born in Mexico, but has been reared in the United States and in American schools. The parents speak Spanish fluently, and they most likely have not mastered English. Hence, their English speaking will demonstrate fragmentation. On the other hand, this client, through ESL education has become fluent with English while remaining fluent in Spanish.

Many Mexicans demonstrate physical traits of American Indians due to the inbreeding of their ancestors with Spanish conquerors. Their Catholic faith was also adopted from Spanish overlords while retaining traits of Aztec spirituality. Spanish nobility alienated them as mestizos. Nevertheless, deep within their souls lives the knowledge and heritage of the ancient Aztec or Mexicas Empire that dominated much of Northern and Central Mexico. In fact, acculturation substantiates the history of Mexican Americans.

African-Americans have a strong ethnic heritage although their ancestors have been enslaved in American territories for 235 years.[2] African-Americans demonstrate the spirit of seeking freedom in the face of oppression and alienation. This is also demonstrated in the spirit of their religious worship and Gospel music, namely, the Spiritual.[3] They emerged from oppression demonstrating segregation from their Caucasian counterparts among the major Protestant denominations, namely, the Methodists, Baptists and Presbyterians, and this was even true within the Roman Catholic Church.[4]

African-American parents demonstrate a wisdom that one only receives through a history of trials and poverty. Traditionally, many African-American youth have gravitated toward the helping professions such as teaching, ministry, social work and counseling. During days of slavery and into the era of Jim Crow, they maintained the homes of their Caucasian counterparts and nurtured Caucasian children while rearing their own children and maintaining their homes.

Interestingly, Martin Luther King may be remembered as "our Moses" in that African-Americans saw him as their God-ordained deliverer in the image of Moses of old. In fact, Moses of Israel liberated the Jews from four hundred years of bondage to the yoke of Pharaoh. Martin Luther King spoke of being on the mountaintop like Moses on Mount Sinai. As Moses saw the Promised Land of Canaan, so Dr. King saw the Day of Liberation for African-Americans, and like Moses, he would not be there with them, as if to say, he would fall asleep in the Lord as did Moses shortly before the liberation of his people.

Today I have observed more African-Americans finding success in the American Dream than in the past. Since being a young man in high school through my current age of 70, I have noted more African-American medical doctors, executives and African-Americans in other positions of leadership apart from those of caregiving. In contrast, many young

African-Americans, whom I counsel, are taking for granted the new world of opportunities in which they now live. In reality, they remain the children of acculturation with the culture of slavery of their ancestors as well as the children of reeducation through predominantly Anglo-American schooling.

African-American youth are being redirected in American culture through exposure to their predominantly African heritage. They are educated into the history of African-American leaders from the days of slavery through the present. They are also educated into their African heritage as it developed in areas like Egypt, Ethiopia and the Central African nations. Essentially, through education, African-Americans are being enculturated from the culture of slavery into the culture of freedom, citizenship and dignity. They are being made aware of their cultural identity and the knowledge base of their history and heritage.

African-Americans are being empowered to face challenges in family and society. They are being renewed in their knowledge base and in personae that are free from estrangement and abasement. Nevertheless, they must still cope with prejudice and racism although laws and policies are in place to protect them. Racism, prejudice, rejection and abasement have become muted in today's society and culture. Many clients of poor and marginal families tend to feel this estrangement the most, especially in school.

Hispanic clients, who are in all probability poor, tend most likely to feel the same estrangement as their

African-American counterparts. These clients tend to "fall through the cracks" at school. For example, when they demonstrate learning problems at school, they most likely are not given the services needed for empowerment to cope and succeed academically. Often their learning issues become behavior issues, and these, in turn, are facilitated by the punitive prejudicial attitudes of school staff.

In contrast, Anglo-Americans demonstrate less problems at school than their African-American and Hispanic American counterparts. Much of the time, Hispanic and African-Americans lose out because their mothers or both parents do not have the education or sophistication to advocate effectively for them. Resultantly, counseling involves my teaching them to advocate or even advocating with them and for them. The role of counselor as advocate usually takes place in school and in court. In the role of counselor and therapist, I am helping my counselees to heal and to succeed.

Anglo-Americans, unlike their Hispanic and African-American counterparts, are often considered well off in comparison. Nevertheless, of the Anglo-American clients that I have worked with, a smaller group of them present as bing poor and marginal, but the vast majority of these clients come from working class families that most likely include the lower, upper lower and lower middle classes. These children like their Hispanic and African-American counterparts receive mental health and substance abuse treatment and services with Medicaid and other state funding.

These clients are mostly of Western European stock. For example, they may be traced to British, Scotch-Irish, Germans, Scandinavians, Spanish, French and Italians. To a lesser extent they are traced to peoples of Eastern Europe and Russia. However, many of these peoples share one principle commonality. They are mostly fair complected and have over the years become enculturated into Anglo-American culture, which in reality is basically British but fragmented with bits and pieces of the other cultures heretofore mentioned.

Of course, this piecing together of fragments results from the American philosophy of assimilation. The closest metaphor reflecting the idea of assimilation refers to the melting pot. In fact, this metaphor became the descriptive applied by Anglo-American society to ethnic immigrants who arrived on their shores. For example, my grandparents and parents believed they had to give up their culture and language to become American, and they instilled that into us. This is quite unlike today's Hispanic immigrants who are encouraged to maintain their language and culture in America. The belief is that Hispanics will acculturate rather than assimilate. In essence, acculturation involves an exchange of cultural traits between ethnic societies. Thus cultural identity is not destroyed but enriched and therefore enhanced.

Anglo-American culture and identity in time will become multicultural and multilingual. However, in the present time, tension exists with the three ethnic groups that make up my clients. (This is not to deny that other ethnic groups in this country are experiencing the same tension, such as Arabs and Greeks in national metropolitan areas, but my focus is on clients and their ethnicities and nationalities.) Seeing myself in the position of a third-generation, Arab-Lebanese American very much assimilated into Anglo-American culture, I find myself caught in the middle. I am feeling the struggle of Anglo-Americans adjusting with and accepting the Hispanic and African-American cultures and the identities of Hispanic and African-American cultures as maintaining their uniqueness in the face of Anglo-American culture and uniqueness.

New immigrants find great difficulty with being unaccepted by Anglo-American society as they refuse to assimilate. For example, Anglo-Americans often criticize Hispanics for not learning the American English language as the characteristic most obvious to social acceptance. At the same time, many Hispanics demonstrate strong traits of mestizo characterizing their dark skin and other American Indian facial and bodily features.

Likewise African-Americans continue to experience the same issues although, over the centuries, many of them are somewhat assimilated into Anglo-American culture (which included interracial marriages and cohabitation). They still retain their brown and black skin colors with other physical traits that characterize their African progenitors. Many African-Americans have maintained their own version of the English language. In fact, some years back an attempt was made to describe that language as Ebonics.⁵ Similarly, the different classes of Anglo-Americans apply their versions of the English language as well. Nevertheless, the more educated of these groups tend to speak and write the formally defined English language.

As noted earlier, the traditional Hispanic American, religious ethic is Roman Catholic, and the African-American religious ethic is an emotional version of Protestantism expressed in the Spiritual. However, in recent years, many Hispanics are adopting the Protestant Evangelical ethos of their Anglo-American counterparts while many among the latter are eating Latin American cuisine, engaging in Latin American culture and history and learning Spanish.

Although, in the United States, significant numbers of Anglo-Americans identify with the Roman Catholic Church, many more identify with the Protestant churches. Even yet, the Protestant Evangelical ethos substantiates the religious heart of many Anglo-Americans. This ethos is based upon European Calvinism and was brought to American shores by many of the European emigrants from England, Germany and Holland. Calvinistic polity also substantiates Congregationalism and Presbyterianism bequeathed by our Puritan forebears and other Calvinistic and Reformed groups. They settled in the Eastern Colonies and then moved west seeking the Manifest Destiny.⁶

Today many Anglo-American clients and parents are unaware of their historic and ethnic identity. Nevertheless, they remain implicitly driven by the traditional belief of America as the chosen and unique City on the Hill standing above the sea while shining its light to all of the lands around it. This uniqueness of America has become an ethos demanding that all conform to it.

All in all, counseling involves facilitating multicultural clients into realizing the value of their uniqueness while guiding them into the acceptance of self and other. Culture, ethnicity, family, nationality, history, language, religions and spiritualty, personality with physical characteristics, and knowledge base with talents, strengths and needs define the uniqueness of clients. Essentially, these diverse personalities reflect the plurality of nations comprising the United States.

Likewise African-American populations are identified regionally in the United States and, transgenerationally, in the plurality of African nations as well as other nations.[7] Also, Hispanic populations are traced to Mexico and other Latin American nations. Historically and culturally, they are traced to Aztec and Incan ancestors while Anglo-American populations are traced to many European and Balkan nations.

Two   Curative Awareness

Three

Infinite Possibilities
Artistic Paradigms

These populations as reflected in each personality demonstrate needs defined in terms of deficits. Clients most likely demonstrate deficits relative to the following issues and disorders. These are mental health, substance abuse, learning, thinking, acculturation[8] especially related to assimilation,[9] adaptation[10] and adjustment, family dysfunction, communication, social skills, social and/or economic status, obsessiveness and compulsiveness, self-concept, dependence and codependence, objectification and alienation. In addition, other deficits may increase while most likely complementing them.

These deficits impact on the wholeness of the personality, which are defined and shaped by cultural and familial contexts. Ethnicity, culture and family shape client personalities, which, in turn, include social contexts of the greater Anglo-American community of schools, church (if not ethnic congregations), corporations and businesses, medical clinics, hospitals, government agencies, mental health and substance abuse agencies and others. Although inclined toward wholeness, personalities in these contexts are often negatively challenged. Many of them result with the imbalance of deficits over sufficits conveying fragmentation in the total composition of the personality.

Herein fragmentation reflects concepts of distortion, imbalance, malformation, asymmetry and the like. In fact, these concepts along with their binary opposites depict in philosophy, language and the arts the key elements of design and artistic composition as well as balance and completeness of being. Likewise in counseling and therapy, client personalities reflect these same concepts. As artist and canvas, composer and composition, clients form personality by either moving it toward togetherness or fragmentation. Counselors as artistic mentors who facilitate the compositions of whole and transformed personalities guide clients as artists.

The common themes of all elements of the fine arts include balance and proportion. In turn, these require cohesiveness of traits comprising each paradigm and metaphor. Essentially, balance and proportion denote wholeness in composition and personality, and overall, being and life. Balance and proportion also provide the esthetic in art, personality and being. That is, beauty is demonstrated in balance, symmetry, continuity, emphasis and proportion. One may refer to the following examples: the sculpture of David by Michelangelo, the Moonlight Sonata by Beethoven, the Last Supper by Leonardo Da Vinci,

Three   Infinite Possibilities

The Raven by Edgar Allen Poe, the Research Tower on the S.C. Johnson &Company campus by Frank Lloyd Wright, and The Great Gatsby by F. Scott Fitzgerald.

All in all, esthetics is defined as one's apprehension of beauty. Beauty is discovered by design. Re've'sz emphasizes esthetics through phenomenological understanding: "Here the decisive thing is the work; that is, the structure, the architecture, the multiplicity and the unity of form; in other words, the art-work as such." [11] One's eyes must be turned outward to grasp the object—the work of art "in its proportions and in its interplay of forces...."[12] The *how* refers to design, and the ability to comprehend design "demands an ability to analyze, a large and varied range of knowledge, a sense feeling for style...."[13]

The key elements of art and design are proposed in that these strongly corroborate the musical elements and the elements of writing and poetry. They also strongly facilitate my understanding of personalities and the art of counseling with them. I have developed "a large and varied range of knowledge," of personalities, namely, the elements or traits that clients convey. This knowledge base facilitates my ability to comprehend the uniqueness and design of each personality. In turn, this empowers effective counseling approaches with clients.

Like the esthetician, I am seeking beauty: that is, the balance, proportion and wholeness of each personality. In seeking beauty, clients are guided in creating the beauty of personality, which includes the wholeness of being. Therefore, through counseling, the elements of art and design are conveyed to client personalities. Clients learn through listening, seeing, feeling and touching as do musicians, writers, painters and sculptors.

Through engaging in the elements, clients apprehend the esthetic of self and being. Some of these are indicated as point, line, form, shape and space, movement, color, pattern and texture. Others are indicated as direction, size and value. Still others are listed as balance, gradation, repetition, contrast, harmony, dominance and unity. The reader may refer to Lovett's picturesque examples of each of the elements[14]

Also, included in the principles and elements of art and design are those of music. I experienced the value and practicality of music as a complementary way of understanding and shaping the personalities of clients. As with art and design, the principles and elements of music are listed. These include dynamics, duration, rhythm, structure, melody, meter, instrumentation, texture, tempo, and timbre.[15] Their structure is emphasized, that is, *how*, the elements of music are arranged and utilized to create works of art and *how* the elements themselves are developed and improved upon. The elements of design are defined and explained in terms of visual art, writing, poetry and music.

We begin with balance or equilibrium. Balance is comprised of two categories. These are symmetry and asymmetry. Symmetry may depict an equal amount of space on both sides of a centerline or hypothetical plumb line. One's perceptive sense would hear balance through the coherence of sound resulting from a balanced application of musical elements. In contrast, asymmetrical balance also referred to as informal or occult depicts the inequality of space or elements existing on both sides of a centerline. Asymmetry prevents monotony and sameness in painting, sculpture, music and literary composition.

Other major elements include continuity, emphasis, and proportion. Through continuity, ideas are connected and developed without a break or interruption. Continuity is depicted by repetition (------------------), alternation (-.-.-.-.-.-.-.) and progression (- -- --- ---- ----- ------). These three devices also illustrate harmony and variety in musical and literary composition.

Through emphasis, ideas along with elements in composition are arranged in terms of dominance and subordination. Some are stressed while others are not, e.g., the dynamic levels in music (^ - ^ - ^ - ^ - ^ - ^ - ^ -).

Proportion includes, symmetry, harmony, and balance. One's esthetic sense perceives a pleasing relationship between ideas of quantity and degree in composition. In music, degrees of tempo may be sensed in comparison to dynamic levels. In all the arts, elements, ideas, shapes and sounds may differ but are connected creating unity and a balanced whole.

Through expression in the arts, sensitivity to "the *value* of the art work" is acquired in that it is "apprehended by the *soul*" and "fully evaluated by the *mind*" [Italics mine]. The work is not created for an emotional experience but to "give expression to …spiritual aims."[16] Substantially, the artist develops a strong intuitive sense. A deep sense regarding the esthetic of design is cultivated. Like the mystic, the artist reaches beyond the intellect without disregarding it to create and value the beauty and wholeness of composition. The artist develops a highly emotional/intellectual sense of heart that rises beyond every-day reason and logic. Rather the heart, the inner source of mind, is empowered with the apprehension of meta-values such as beauty, love and truth. Obviously, this is the spiritual end of human soul, being and art.

Resultantly, through the arts, students and counselors develop the intuitive sense of being and principles of design in being. They develop a strong sense of style, proportion, balance and unity. As highly cultivated human ears and eyes discern and apprehend the mystery of beauty in art, so writers, poets, performers, composers, and painters intuitively apprehend ideas flowing from the heart through their particular media. Likewise counselors highly skilled with clients are empowered to sense the insensible and to know the unknowable. Such professionals with highly cultivated hearts see either the beauty of wholeness in the client's personality or the imbalance and dysfunction of that personality.

Overall, counselors and artists acquire the domain of knowledge of their arts analytically. Jerome Brunner posits: "intuitive thinking rests on familiarity with the domain of knowledge involved and with its structure."[17] Acquiring, for example, the knowledge of music structurally may be accomplished through the explicit step-by-step process characterizing analytic thinking. At the same time, art is applied through ontological contact with a medium such as pen and paper, the piano, paint, charcoal and canvas or the body as in dance. Like the arts, counseling also has its medium, namely, the ontological contact of the counselors and clients with personalities of self and other.

At the same time, counselors see clients analytically and apply palates of varied therapies in order to elicit new compositions. In doing so, they empower their clients with the technical facility to assess and recompose personality. Over time, through miming the traits of the counselor as artist, clients become self-directed artists of self and personality. This step-by-step learning process engaged in by counselors and clients evolves through clients' cultivation of counselors' analytical and intuitive personae. In other words, clients acquire the domain of self-knowledge as well as experiencing counselors' knowledge of self and personality, counseling methods and theory, and other theoretical and experiential knowledge.

Overall, effective counseling requires a strong analytically intuitive sense, and this, in turn, corroborates a strong ability to hypothesize regarding the personality, needs and treatment of clients. For the sake of substantiating this self-study, knowledge and learning relative to intuition are being corroborated by perceptual inferring. Levine writes: when people perceive, they take information received through the senses and organize it into meaningful wholes. These wholes become patterns or configurations called gestalts.

For example, in music, counseling and any other body of knowledge, one aspect of the whole (pattern) may be a datum or data called percepts. In turn, percepts synthesize to form meaningful wholes called concepts while, in turn, concepts synthesize into multiplex wholes to form generalizations. Levine postulates that people often arrange data or specifics into groups under the categories of continuity and similarity.[18] Two objects side by side with the same shape or are mirroring one another may depict similarity.[19] Continuity, as illustrated above, is also defined as the continuation of a thing or idea over time and space without interruption. It depicts two or more similar things or ideas that connect.[20] Continuity depicts the flow of logic in writing, music and painting.

Through similarity and continuity, people organize their worlds in terms of gestalts. They synergize thoughts, images, ideas, feelings and experiences into a whole.[21] This whole is the summation of varied yet related parts, but differs from the synergizing of its parts. In music, art and writing, differences are often interrelated as similarities to support a theme or center of interest.

Melody in music is comprised of small units called motifs. The Fifth Symphony of Beethoven (First Movement) provides an apt example of one motif demonstrating similarity and continuity thematically and developmentally. In all of the arts, motifs form patterns that convey relationship and connectedness.[22]

As the psyche passes through life, the autobiography[23] is formed through continuity and similarity. The gestalt of worldview is created and personality characteristics are formed relative to autobiographical experience and worldview. The composition of self and person are formed. As the psyche learns, many gestalts are formed and synergized creating one inclusive gestalt. However, as in forming a body of knowledge, gaps are left. This is especially apparent in concept formation and generalization.

Forming a body of knowledge may be likened to the formation of the worldview as the autobiography conveys the knowledge of one's worldview. Likewise through the process of acquiring familiarity with a body of knowledge, gestalts are formed, but in the process gaps are left.

In the stream of consciousness, gaps are left. In the maturing learner, impulses arising from knowledge acquired send a message arousing an experience of discomfort and/or curiosity. The learner, through analytic thinking, research and study, fills in the gap. In regarding the esthetic, the listener senses perfect balance and proportion in the music elements of a composition. Most likely, the listener cannot explain the esthetic in words but knows intuitively because of previous and extensive involvement in the elements of music and principles of design. The listener's gaps are verbal so he or she will reflect back analytically and strive to explain *what* is sensed.

Levine refers to the filling in of gaps as perceptual inference. Fundamentally, we perceive "what our senses tell us." However, we experience much in living that is either missed or forgotten. In this case, perceptual inference becomes "largely automatic and unconscious." At recall, cues will arouse our consciousness to what was lost through forgetting. At the same time, we sense familiarity with things, persons and places forgotten or lost in the past. In dreams, we will recall the unknown and forgotten. Perceptual inference provides the clue to intuitiveness.[24]

Through the gaps of consciousness, the unconsciousness will come into play. Through composing music, a strongly melodic idea is sensed allowing the musician to often automatically hear or play the composition through. Through counseling, the stream of autobiographical experience opens gaps for intuitiveness relative to meeting new clients and assessing needs and strengths. Having a strong ethnic upbringing provides insight and intuitiveness into clients' cultural experiences, needs, strengths and behaviors. Many hypotheses for treatment are derived through strong multicultural, spiritual, philosophical, anthropological and counseling knowledge and autobiographical experience.

Autobiography and Art

From experiencing the arts, my knowledge and experience with counseling and personality interface with the elements of personality both in terms of client deficits relative to needs and client strengths, namely, sufficits. Of course, elements that make up the personality are vast and numerous, but the client as psyche reaches into the world of self and creates a personality with deficits and sufficits.[25] These, in turn, give shape to the autobiography of the client, which becomes the mirror of personality attributes and worldview. Autobiography reflects the client's story of life that includes successes and failures with negative and positive experiences. The autobiography discloses personality deficits and sufficits, and these give diagnostic cues for treatment interventions.

At the same time, culture and ethnicity as well as family, school and community shape the autobiographies of clients. Therapeutic listening indicates the recognition of behavioral cues that allow insight into clients' personalities and worldviews. Connecting with clients effectively, in the sense of Carl Rogers, involves unconditional positive regard.[26] Listening includes empathy with reflectiveness and providing a sense of home. This sense engenders a context of safety and belongingness. Resultantly, clients experience the freedom to share their stories.

Therapeutic listening recognizes and affirms strengths, which appear as sufficits, while trying to modify deficits and needs into strengths. Listening and reflecting convey trust and facilitate communication.

Many who come for therapy no longer trust. Genuine positive regard opens the door of the counselor's personality so that positive attributes such as trust may be conveyed to clients and, in turn, elicited from them. Clients are permitted to see in the counselor's personality, the Rogerian concepts of respect, congruence, and acceptance. The therapeutic vision of counseling perceives clients as becoming whole persons and empowered to blossom into the most beautiful of flowers. This *terminus* of counseling strongly reflects Abraham Maslow's self-actualization, Deldon McNeely's becoming and Carl Jung's individuation.[27]

In fact, the above concepts may be seen as catalysts that convey positive traits in therapy sessions. Through the experience of counseling, I often relate to clients as I did piano students. My piano students begin learning basic five-finger exercises while working on their hand positions. They were guided to focus on quality of tone as coming from the bottom of the keys of the piano. They were taught to let their fingers carry the weight of their arms and hands and eventually their whole bodies. Each tone is produced by this weight falling into each finger.

Likewise clients, in the initial stages of counseling, are guided into relaxing with self and context. Clients learn to sense the depth of belonging allowing them ease with engaging in counseling. Clients are given the respect and delicacy conveyed to piano students. Clients are given a sense of self and personality as with the musical instrument and the power to draw beauty from them. In the process of learning the piano, the young musician begins to listen and feel the emotions behind each tone. Clients are guided into listening to self and feeling thoughts and emotions relative to self and world.

In these early beginnings, piano students ease into learning by translating basic tones into simple melodies, and clients ease into translating basic thoughts and emotions into simple stories of their individual history. These stories reflect the autobiography and composite personality traits.

Unlike piano students, who begin learning basic notes, tone and melody, counselees began learning the basics of the instrument of personality and the meaning of their personal symbols. This learning continues through environmental interactions and responses, which influence the stages of human development through life.

My clients begin engaging in counseling during the "turbulence" of adolescent development. More or less, they indicate an imbalance of deficits over sufficits in the personality somewhat as previous teachers incorrectly taught their piano students. Regarding both students and clients, I provide genuine positive regard while giving encouragement and understanding in basic piano teaching and the counseling process.

Interestingly, the piano teacher in reality is considered a piano pedagogue. In ancient Greek and Roman cultures, the idea of pedagogue was of teaching and caring for the whole person as disciple.[28] The pedagogue was a nurturer. Hence, this concept of piano pedagogue was passed to musicians from Russia through the piano teaching of Madame and Leon Conus. As a pianist, I consider myself fortunate to have studied in that tradition.

Reflectively, this tradition is translated into counseling and therapy. Seeing myself as mentor, facilitator, caregiver, guide, and teacher, I work with the whole person, the ontology of their existence. This includes the being and psyche of clients including mind, spirit, body, and personality. Total being involves the contexts of clients and their impact on personality characteristics. Contexts also include ethnicity, culture, race, language, and family.

In fact, the whole being of the person may be summed up in the personality. Specifically, personality depicts the individuality and uniqueness of the person. In addition, this person is reflected in autobiography much of which is gathered beginning with the Comprehensive Clinical Assessment. From this point, client stories are expanded through therapeutic sessions and recorded in case notes with supplementary data being included in the client chart.

Art and Design, Expository Writing and Music

Paradigmatically, personality is being reflected in several basic sketches. These of course include autobiography, culture and ethnicity, and traits of the fine arts.

Culture:

Along with race and ethnicity, culture depicts the paradigm and substance of the personality. This includes physical traits, religion and spirituality, language, mannerisms, worldview and perspective. "Culture refers to the cumulative deposit of knowledge, experience, beliefs, values, attitudes, meanings, hierarchies, religion, notions of time, roles, spatial relations, concepts of the universe, and material objects and possessions acquired by a group of people in the course of generations through individual and group striving"[29]

Balance and Harmony:

Traits of an individual demonstrate proportion and interconnectedness. The traits of the body demonstrate proportion in the direct shape of the male and in the curvilinear shape of the female, yet allowing weight to be distributed evenly permitting the person to stand and walk upright. Traits demonstrate themselves in attitudes and behaviors with logic and interrelatedness. All virtues are interconnected and display characterological balance and harmony. Vices in contrast, create the opposite of balance and harmony.

Nevertheless, all human beings are usually caught between the two categories. Harmony as in music demonstrates agreement and connectedness through the pleasing sounds of musical notes produced by chords and chord progressions that are interrelated and working themselves out into a theme. Of course, the opposites of balance and harmony include those of imbalance as in dissonance and cacophony. These demonstrate the brokenness of the whole through fragmentation and incompleteness. While harmony and balance demonstrate categories of sufficits, their opposites demonstrate deficits in the personality as in a composition.[30]

Tone/Tonality/Timbre/Instrumentation:

The quality of sound or emotion is conveyed by a work of art, music and writing. The human personality may display itself as flat, bright, pathos, sad, angry, funny, somber, and labile among others. In art, color combinations create tones from warm to cold colors. In music, tones are demonstrated through minor to major melodic and harmonic progressions conveying pathos, anger, storminess, brightness and joyfulness. Color like music may also display dissonance and cacophony through the application of clashing color and harmonic progressions. Musical instruments are combined in ways that convey tone, timbre, and tonality, which create color and depth. Likewise, the traits of personality work together conveying the said qualities.

Dominance/Contrast/Variation/Repetition/Dynamics:

A work of art or a composition demonstrates the following traits and their opposites. These are dominance and subordination, comparison and contrast, variation and repetition, and dynamics and stasis. Dynamics relate to process and variation in life. In literature, the dynamics of a character refers to the life and personality traits of the character. In music, dynamics refers to the life of music as being in louds and softs, crescendos and diminuendos, retards and accelarandos the movement and development of music. The same may be said of art and poetry. Stasis, in contrast, conveys monotony and stagnancy such as personality displaying a flat affect. Stasis, as opposed to dynamic, demonstrates traits of boredom, lack of interest or motivation, goalessness and other similarities. A dynamic personality exhibits the opposite traits. Such a person tends to be involved, enthusiastic, goal oriented, and invested.

In visual art, comparison/contrast demonstrates dominant and subordinate themes with lines, shapes, and colors exist to create variation and repetition. This is true with the thematic and tonal structure of music. Literary characters, themes and poetic metaphors and stanzas also demonstrate traits of dominance, subordination, repetition and variation. Human personalities demonstrate these traits physically, emotionally and culturally. In literature and writing, especially, comparison/contrast demonstrates the dynamics of thematic and conceptual development. Comparison/contrast is suggested and implied in the color and dynamic gradations as well as with lines and shapes in art and design. In music, comparison/contrast is suggested in thematic and tonal similarities as well as in the dynamics of melody and harmony. Music suggests repetition and variation thematically, in melodic and harmonic structure as well as in tonality and dynamics. All aforementioned nuances are noted in the life of a healthful and whole human personality.

Rhythm/Meter/Duration/Tempo/Emphasis

Human personalities demonstrate rhythm through walking, talking, running, singing, playing musical instruments and dancing. Rhythm is demonstrated in the display of varied traits, clothing tastes and food preferences as reflecting family and culture. All traits together convey a variety and repetition in patterns and suggest tendencies. In dance, music, writing and poetry, duration is suggested in pauses, whole, half and quarter notes depending on tempo, fermatas, punctuation, choreographed dance steps and stress on particular colors, lines and shapes. Of course, in music and poetry, meter sets the pace for tempo markings such as duple, quadruple, etc. which includes strong accents followed by weak accents in metrics such as duple, triple, quadruple, etc. Even in expository writing, all of the aforesaid elements contribute to rhythm and emphasis. Ideas, concepts and sentences are delineated through parallelism, repetition, variation and elaboration.

Unity/Structure/Coherence/Texture

Unity and structure relate very much to balance and harmony. "A principle of art, *unity* occurs when all of the elements of a composition combine to make a balanced, harmonious and complete *whole*. Unity is another of those hard-to-describe art terms but when it is present, both eye and brain are pleased to see it."[31] At the same time, unity refers to the components of the many joining together to make one. This is further illustrated in the following definition from Google: "the arrangement of and relations between the parts or elements of something complex."[32] Hence, the diverse elements mentioned above conjoin into a structural whole. Together these create texture. Texture denotes the appearance of interwoven elements such as the interwoven fibers of a tapestry.[33]

Also, all of the components of structural unity demonstrate clarity of thesis, theme, and structure like a literary or musical composition demonstrating a beginning middle and end. Furthermore, all components comprising beginning, middle, and end are joined together by a development. Implicitly, in art, the theme is the center of interest and all other images join together to enhance the center of interest.

Likewise, the personality is centered on a theme or center of interest. This aspect of personality traits appeals to the beholder in ontological contact, and depending on the gravity and power of the theme—this most likely engenders the charismatic appeal of some personalities. In writing, all ideas are logically conjoined through appropriate word choice, sentence and paragraph structure. In contrast, deficits in personality, as in written and spoken language, would be illogical and fragmentary. Relatively, deficits in writing and speaking reflect disorders in speech and writing.

Poetic Symbols and Devices

Pertinent to personality are clients' usage of language and its structure, which, in turn, is most likely reflective of culture and family rearing. Clients speak differently, utilizing varied word choices and orders. Their language, writing and speech contain what anthropologists call key metaphors or symbols reflecting their culture, family, and age group. Many clients apply symbols relating to a particular group, gang or favorite drug. Some clients demonstrate polish in speaking and writing. Polish is noted in less fractured and more logical and articulated talk and writing than others produce.

Hispanic gang members will often wear a rosary, which is symbolic of their Catholic-Latino heritage. For example, Our Lady of Guadalupe is the key metaphor of Mexico. She not only is linked with the Catholic heart of Mexican culture but the Mexicas heart as well. She is related to Tonantzin, the Aztec Earth Goddess called Our Reverend Mother.[34]

In counseling, I listen carefully for poetic devices as these define the personality and culture of clients. African-American male clients continue to be reared by their mothers and grandmothers. One side of them is struggling for freedom as conveyed in African-American Spirituals, yet they remain dominated by the care of the Mother figure (a very strong image in African-American culture) for whom they struggle with out of both respect and resistance.[35] Many often end up in the juvenile justice system, which most likely provides the dominant male, father figure for them.[36]

Another male figure close to African-American boys is the Minister figure, as with Martin Luther King. The minister is the redemptive figure for African-Americans. In fact, so important is the minister figure to them, that the wife of the minister is called the First Lady. In fact, a title for the pastor's wife is typical of ethnic churches. For example, the priest's wife in Eastern Orthodoxy is called *Presbytera* while the priest is called *Presbyter*.

In counseling, I have begun to postulate an emergent male role model This is summed up in the star athlete as demonstrated through stars such as Michale Jordan, Mohammed Ali, and Tiger Woods. Becoming a sports star is the dream shared among many African American male clients.

In talking with clients, I listen for metaphors, symbols, personifications, irony, idiom, hyperbole and other devices mentioned above. Caucasian clients, while still implicitly dominated by the Calvinistic heritage, are struggling with identity relative to ontological contact with the identities of African-American and Hispanic American peers. Some Anglo-American clients have conveyed the prejudice of school staff toward their cultural counterparts, while others feel confusion and resentment toward them. At the same time, even others accept their cultural counterparts as peers, acquaintances and friends.

In considering personality traits, speech and writing convey uniqueness of personality and being. Some basic poetic devices are discussed as follows:

Imagery/Metaphor/Symbol/Personification/Tone

Clients may speak and write in word combinations as defined by their culture, family, schooling and interactions. In counseling, clients' apply images as symbols, namely, images representing something else. This is obviously demonstrated in art, for example, the house-tree-person drawing. Clients also, demonstrate tonality especially through, mood relative to imagery in art and language. Metaphors paradigmatically depict symbols of happiness, sadness, flatness and the like. Clients also express tone in terms of personification, that is, giving human qualities to other living and nonliving things in nature and being.

Hyperbole/Allegory/Simile/Idiom/Irony

Other devices conveyed by clients include thoughts and feelings in terms of tone such as exaggeration to convey images or ideas. Clients often exaggerate experiences for the sake of self-justification. They choose particular words and order them in such a way even to the point of illogic in order to elicit positive support from authority figures. They do this despite the gravity of mistaken decisions and actions taken from the start. Such expressions may either be idiomatic, hyperbolic or both.

At the same time, counseling involves listening for the possible implicit meaning behind apparent concrete language. Generally, human beings tend toward allegory in the flow of language. For example, if clients experienced abuse earlier or even recently in life, their "concrete language" may implicitly convey the most likelihood of abuse. Angry and untrusting clients may display irony in terms of sarcasm and/or exaggeration.

Onomatopoeia/Alliteration/Assonance

In reflective listening with clients, these devices occur not as often as others mentioned above, yet they do occur every now and then through writing. With alliteration, clients repeat the first consonant sound in a group of words.[37] For example: "Love's labours lost," and I by fault, fought, [then] fled. With assonance, clients repeat vowel sounds in the flow of words such as glade, blaze. grace. daze, etc. (See citation as another example.)[38] Some clients have applied onomatopoeia through animal sounds, such as moo, maah, bah, ribbit, cock-a-doodle-do, tse-e-e. oink, chirp, cheep, hiss, etc. Clients and I have role played in fun acting like animals.[39] These devices set tone and mood.

Diction/Word Order

Above, we noted that word order and its pronunciation varies from client to client. Diction refers to word order based on syntax, i.e., rules of grammar relating to the formation of sentences. Factors considered during therapy include culture, education level, socioeconomic status and intelligence level. Also considered are developmental delays, specific mental health issues and other education problems that impact on diction and word order.

Denotation and Connotation

Clients, through spoken and written language, often define concepts and ideas indirectly in terms of allusions, connotations and implications. In contrast, clients also define concepts directly and exactly as suggested by the concept denotation. Clients tend to define experiences indirectly. For instance, if a parent asks an adolescent where he or she is going, the adolescent most likely answers, "out" or "to hang out." He or she avoids stating what he or she is exactly doing, such as "going to the movie " or "going to Johnny's house." Through counseling, I usually listen closely for connotative meanings and descriptives over and against denotative meanings and descriptives.

Overall, I consider all artistic and literary elements together to facilitate understanding the autobiographical personality of clients. Together these elements provide guides demarking personality sufficits and deficits, while mentoring clients toward wholeness. Of course, definitions of deficits are also therapeutically considered in the DSM V. Laying hold on deficits and sufficits in terms of the elements of arts and literature, empowers clients as artists to gain control of personality, life and being by moving these from fragmentation to wholeness.

Three   Infinite Possibilities

Four

Contemporary Personality Theory
Trait Theory

In essence, all of these paradigmatic metaphors become ways of summarizing the thousands of traits that comprise the human personality. In fact, Gordon Allport[53] concluded that several thousand traits comprised the personality. This is most likely as personality mirrors the autobiography, which is shaped by one's cultural, familial, physical, mental, psychological, and spiritual being. Allport broke these down into classifications emphasizing varying dimensions of dominant and subordinate traits. However, other psychologists following him such as Raymond Cattell[54], Hans Eysenek[55] and Donald W. Fiske[56] attempted to summarize these traits for the sake of measuring. Interestingly, they arranged personality traits into key binary oppositions emphasizing emotional and psychological balance and harmony as opposed to imbalance and dissonance. They applied the paradoxical frameworks of both/and and either/or. Both/and usually indicated balance and harmony of thinking and emotions while either/or indicated imbalance and even dissonance of thinking and emotions. Either/or concepts such as the following would include many subsets or categories, as extroversion/introversion, neurotic/calm, open/closed, and labile/stable.

Although the writer would prefer not to, for the sake of abbreviation, Fiske's quintuple system of summarizing personality traits is being applied to the three personality sketches ahead. Fiske labeled these as follows:

>Closed/Open,
>
>Spontaneous/Conscientious
>
>Introversion/Extroversion
>
>Hostile/Agreeable
>
>Neurotic/Stable

Each of these concepts is multifaceted well expressing such traits as balance/imbalance, warm/cold, caring/selfish, generous/stingy, consonant/dissonant, grim/bright, quiet/loud, large/small, educated/uninformed, involved/uninvolved, slow/fast, staid/frivolous, and insightful/unperceptive. Of the quintuple scale: (1) *openness* includes traits of brightness, understanding, philosophical, creative and artistic. In contrast, *closed* includes traits of dullness, unperceptive or insensitivity to the other, concrete or irrational, sterile or unimaginative, and uncreative. (2) *Conscientious* refers to traits of diligence, completeness, reliability and faithful. In contrast, *spontaneous* refers to traits impulsive, careless, irresponsible, and inexact. (3) *Extroversion* indicates traits of social openness and even gregariousness; whereas, *introversion* indicates social closedness and even introvertedness. (4) *Agreeableness* refers to traits described as trusting, kind, considerate, compassionate and pleasant; whereas, *hostile* or hostility indicates enmity, unkindness, inconsiderateness, uncaring or merciless, and disagreeable or cold. (5) *Neurotic* is indicative of traits such as irritable, moody, nervous and temperamental. In contrast, *stable* or stability refers to such traits as pleasant, nice or joyous, balanced or cheerful, calm, composed or confident, and predictable, reliable, steady and trustworthy.

Also, these traits cross cultures. In terms of the many dimensions of dominance and subordination, physical and cultural traits may be identified in terms of skin color, language, body build, shared feelings, attitudes and values, talents, strengths and needs and tastes in dress, color and design. As the colors on an artist's palate, primary colors when mixed create secondary colors and these in turn create tertiary colors. At the same time, each hue may gradate from black, the deepest dark through white the highest white.

As with personality traits, hues are multifaceted enhancing shapes and line as shadow on canvas.

Differences and contrasts are conjoined creating a unique composition of meaning. As with the deficits/sufficits of each human personality, negative/positive traits are synergized through dominance/subordination while conveying a theme or center of interest.

From a linguistic standpoint, one's psychocultural perceptions consist of binary opposites. Fiske ingenuously applied this to his quintuple system of personality analysis.

Thus in approaching the three personality sketches, one may determine the key personality traits related on both sides of the binary opposition and the gradations in terms of numerical intervals between them. * For example, in applying one category of the quintuple scale, we note the following personality indicating that he or she is both extroverted and introverted. With the application of the Likert scale of 0-10, the following traits of introversion/extroversion indicates a median of 5/10 and the measure of 4/10 indicates that despite the strength of the client's extroversion he or she displays a tendency toward extroversion.

EXTROVERSION

| Introversion | 0 | 1 | 2 | 3 | **4** | 5 |
| 6 | 7 | 8 | 9 | 10 | Extroversion | |

However, from the autobiographies of clients, I have trouble applying these categories although they exist. In summations, they apparently limit the full picture of personality and its intricacies. In looking on the Internet, Ideonomy lists 638 traits, categorized as positive traits (234 = 37%), neutral traits (292 = 18%) and negative traits (292 = 46%).[57] Ideonomy comes from the French Encyclopedic School and denotes the science of ideas.[7] This is not a psychological listing, but bears consideration. Be that as it may, because of the complexity of autobiography, I lean to Gordon Allport's findings indicating several thousand personality traits in the human being.

Personality traits interreflect with the many colors on the artist's palate. They also depict the many tone colors in music writing and poetry. The elements of design, music, poetry and written composition summarize these tones and colors produced through words, musical notation, multiplex sounds, colors and tone gradations, Hence, the following elements of fine art may be summarized demonstrating wholeness and balance in art as well as human personality. Consideration is given to symmetry/asymmetry, proportion/disproportion, balance/imbalance, unity/disunity, coherence/incoherence, and harmony/dissonance. They most likely may be applied with subcategories to all arts and human personalities.

"Nevertheless, in the following personality studies, Fiske's Quintuple personality trait system is being applied.

Five

Three Personality Sketches

Here are three autobiographies of former clients. They represent three cultural groups; Hispanic American, African-American, and Anglo-American Caucasian. These adolescent males have represented much of my counseling experience over the years. Their personality traits and elements reflect the elements and traits of autobiography.[1] In turn, the worldview depicts the gestalt or work of art reflecting autobiography and personality. In this light, the means are being substantiated through which I am able to facilitate and mentor clients as artists and composers of their personalities.

Before proceeding, however, the following sample of my client caseload 534 clients counseled since I began at Insight Human Services. This sample was extracted from a population of 756 clients, which I was able to uncover from even a larger number of clients counseled. The sample represents the majority of my population being males of school age representing three cultural groups, namely, Caucasian=American, African-American and Hispanic American. The population difference represents minorities comprising my client population. This is not only made up some males of the said cultures but principally females of the said cultures as well as males and females of other cultural groups. My rationale for presenting this information is to substantiate my experience with data and relating it to three recent, cultural, personality cases chosen. These exemplify the three major cultural groups with whom I have provided counseling and therapy.

An Anglo American Personality

A young Anglo-American boy is plagued with depression and anxiety. He is 15 years of age and in the tenth grade. The local adolescent psychiatric unit of his community's major medical center referred him for treatment. He was in impatient treatment at this medical center for eight days. He had threatened suicide while going through an episode of major depression. He was diagnosed with marijuana intoxication to the point of experiencing episodes of panic attack, extreme depression, and passing out.

Prior to this, he had successfully completed a wilderness camp program before resuming his experimentation with marijuana and ending up in the hospital. He appears as talkative and open. He is dressed cleanly and neatly in jeans, leather hiking shoes and a white tee shirt. His hair is cut very short, but not as short as a buzz cut. He is built rather broad with muscularity and is of average height for his age.

He loves fishing, hunting and music. He plays piano, trumpet and clarinet. He taught himself piano and has studied these other instruments in band class at school. He does not have a girlfriend, but has several male peers with whom he "hangs out."

He lives in an adjacent rural county. His father presents as a working class gentleman employed by the city in water works. Father displays some coarseness but is very friendly and is seeking help for his son. The boy's mother was with him at the intake and assessment. The father has been involved in some of his son's therapy sessions. The boy and father demonstrate a positive relationship, but the boy demonstrates expressions of displeasure at some comments of the father about his person. The boy demonstrates much sensitivity to his father's comments even if they are positive, but the boy, overall, is respectful and accepting of his mother and father.

At the assessment, his mother described the family as Protestant Christian having been involved in evangelical churches over the years. Currently, he is not active in church and is in the process of questioning the need for belonging to a church. He has not renounced his Christian beliefs, however.

He claims he has some friends that he "hangs out" with; this is not on a daily basis. The client spends much of his time alone involved with music and instrumental practice. He fishes and hunts when he can. Currently, he wants to graduate from high school, but he is not sure of what to do beyond high school. He admits that although he wants to complete high school, he does not really enjoy being there nor does he really want to get up in the morning and attend school. He forces himself to attend school even though he disagrees with doing so.

Having listened to him reflectively, I came to the conclusion that the client most likely is suffering from social anxiety. He admits that he cannot stand to be around large crowds of peers in his classes. He admits that he tends to shut down, thereby, not permitting him to function with effectiveness academically or socially. Nevertheless, he does admit that in classes of interest he is not as fearful as in classes of no interest. Of course, he is somewhat comfortable in his band class because he receives individual attention from the band instructor, but in math and English he will have a rougher time. He feels a little better in social studies, but overall, he experiences fear and anxiety in each of his classes. Resultantly, he is hindered from doing his most effective work and functioning overall.

The client speaks well and is very articulate. However, his spoken language does not demonstrate the polish of an educated person, but does demonstrate the tongue of a common, every-day young man of high school age.

Five   Three Personality Sketches

OPENNESS

Closed 0 1 2 3 4 5 6 **7** 8 9 10   Open

CONSCIENTIOUSNESS

Spontaneous 0 1 2 3 4 5 6 7 **8** 9 10   Conscientious

EXTROVERSION

Introversion 0 1 2 3 **4** 5 6 7 8 9 10   Extroversion

AGREEABLENESS

Hostile 0 1 2 3 4 5 6 7 8 9 10   Agreeable

NEUROTICISM

Neurotic 0 1 2 3 4 5 **6** 7 8 9 10   Stable

An Anglo-American client in counseling demonstrates the following estimates. He indicates the level of 6/10 toward stability, which places him at 6 intervals from neurotic. The client demonstrates the level 9/10 toward agreeableness, which places him at 8 intervals from neurotic. He also shows the level 4/10 toward extroversion, which demonstrates 4 intervals from introversion. The client exhibits the level 7/10 on conscientiousness, which places him at 7 intervals from spontaneous, and he exhibits the level 7/10 toward openness, which places him at 7 intervals from closed. Except for extroversion, all of his trait levels indicate the client as above 5/10, the median of each scale. His personality health indicates average to above average, but the client demonstrates the risk of neuroticism due to his level of 6/10 on that scale, and his stronger tendency from extraversion to introversion is indicated by the level 4/10 on that scale.

Dominant tendencies toward the asymmetry of imbalance and fragmentation are indicated with deficits of introversion and neuroticism. Due to anxiety and depression, especially anxiety, the client may resort to self-medication with marijuana, which does not agree with him. The client, through using marijuana, experiences panic attacks, sleeplessness and major depression. Stressors of school challenges in both academic and social realms threaten the client. His negative, dominant traits of introversion and anxiety are in tension with his positive, dominant traits of musical talent and his love of the outdoors. Another positive, dominant trait is communicating well especially when he feels a sense of belonging and acceptance. Another negative, dominant trait is the tendency to be overly sensitive to what his parents and most likely other adults may say to him, especially, if they do not intend harm to him.

The client's personality, evidently, demonstrates balance and harmony. The tone of his personality is peasant in that he desires to be receptive to others around him. The therapeutic plan for the client is that he continue in counseling weekly to twice per month and that he receive a psychiatric evaluation and be involved in medication therapy once monthly. Care for this client is preventative, and the end and means of counseling and therapy is empowering the Client with skills that shape his personality and worldview holistically.

An African-American Personality

An African-American male of 17 through 18 years of age has been in outpatient treatment for approximately one-and-a-half years. He is currently a junior in high school and is a basketball star there. He stands 5'10" in height and is lean and muscular. He claims to have played basketball since childhood. The client admits to grades being lower than they should in school and believes that he could do better but somehow does not bring himself to that point. His grades most likely are below a cumulative average of 2.0.

The client experiences a close relationship with his basketball coach and is well liked by teachers and peers. He also presents as a pleasant young man with a friendly smile. He presents as handsome with self-assuredness. He reports involvement with his family at church on Sundays and claims the Christian faith. He entered treatment through a school referral due to being under the influence of marijuana. He indicated use "every other day" and continued this pattern 4 to 6 months before entering treatment. He has continued marijuana use over the months while in treatment without yielding a negative drug screen.

The client's mother indicates a history of depression and heart disease, and due to financial difficulties, she and the client live with the maternal grandmother. The client also reports his paternal and maternal grandfathers as dependent on drugs and his father as dependent on crack cocaine. He often worries about his mother and her economic and health problems. Due to low income, the family is unable to live in a safe neighborhood. Nevertheless, the client and family are close.

The client indicates no history of school behavior issues except for a most recent three-day, out-of-school suspension for a marijuana use citation by school staff. Mother also reports, although the client has many friends, many of them will take advantage of him, and some of them are not good for him. Mother reports the client as experiencing normal birth and delivery and meeting all developmental milestones on time.

Five   Three Personality Sketches

The client is diagnosed with Cannabis Abuse, Depressive Disorder Not Otherwise Specified and ADHD-Combined Type, all being by history. The client was in outpatient treatment mental health for several years prior to his admission at Insight. The agency psychiatrist also confirms these diagnoses. Prior to seeing this psychiatrist, the client was treated with Focalin and Zoloft. The psychiatrist took the client off of Focalin due to marijuana use and is maintained on Zoloft modified to 100 mgs/day.

OPENNESS

Closed   0   1   2   3   4   5   6   **7**
          8   9   10   Open

CONSCIENTIOUSNESS

Spontaneous   0   1   2   3   4   5
6   7   **8**   9   10   Conscientious

EXTROVERSION

Introverted   0   1   2   3   **4**   5   6
7   8   9   10   Extroverted

AGREEABLENESS

Hostile   0   1   2   3   4   5   6
7   8   **9**   10   Agreeable

NEUROTICISM

Neurotic   0   1   2   3   4   5   **6**
7   8   9   10   Stable

The client indicates dominance regarding his athletic gifts and as a competitive basketball player. He tends to be gregarious and well liked. These traits are displayed at the level of 9.4/10 on the agreeableness continuum. At the same time, the client indicates the level 9/10 in that he is active, talkative and energetic. He indicates conscientiousness at the level 8/10 with traits of being neat in his appearance and orderly and practical in his manner and outlook. In contrast though, on the openness continuum, he is ranked at 7.3/10 indicating a lower high average than his glaring traits of agreeableness and extroversion.

Underscoring the positive traits of agreeableness and extraversion are creativity and brightness, which strongly depict a talented athlete. Probably underscoring the low high trait of openness is the weak trait of neuroticism as indicated at 4/10. Due to depression and ADHD, the client displays dominant traits of moodiness, irritability, insecurity and temperamentalness. Such symptoms would justify the client's probable use of marijuana for self-medication.

The client's harmony of positive and dominant personality traits tend toward imbalance. This asymmetry is displayed by traits of ADHD and depression, which impact on his brightness and creativity. These antitheses pull on his positive traits especially on his weaker ability toward openness and may even, in turn, impact on his strong tendencies toward extroversion, agreeableness and conscientiousness.

Due to depression and ADHD, the client may even experience periods in which his dominant weak trait related to openness will pull on his strong traits to the point of the client's having clashes with family members and internal struggles with self and others. The client's tone of brightness and personableness may dim into tones of sadness, avoidance and anger. This is especially true, when he finds himself internally struggling to maintain agreeableness, conscientiousness and extroversion. The client continues to struggle for the balance and centrality of positively dominant traits over and against the tendency of negatively dominant traits..

What becomes really harmful for this athlete is that neurotic traits may drain the client of energy, thereby, impacting on the effectiveness of his performance as a basketball player. His coach and family see his weaknesses. In light of this, they provide security and support for the client over and against his sensitivities and shortcomings. His coach also protects him. Somehow the client continues to play ball despite his periods of low grades. At the same time, in the face of family and client struggles, family and coach present with the gleaming hope that this young man is surely to become a basketball star and that such stardom will deliver this family from their current woes of poverty and economic insecurity.

A Hispanic American Personality

We are considering a Hispanic-American male of 13-years of age. He is in the seventh grade at a local middle school. He presents as handsome with a pleasantly sweet disposition. His school recently referred him for treatment. The client was caught on school grounds allegedly selling marijuana to peers and, in turn, was suspended for five days. Nevertheless, the police learned that peers set the client up so that they would avoid blame. They had built a homemade pipe for marijuana use. The client recently completed an alternative school program for demonstrating behavior issues related to marijuana. He abstained from marijuana for one month, but has now failed the drug test twice. Since the incident of selling, the police continue to warn him of possible charges.

Because the client was sharing his fear of school, I referred him to the agency psychiatrist for an evaluation. The client and mother with his 18-year-old cousin, as interpreter, informed the physician that the client had no trouble with depression or anxiety. Consequently, the physician assessed the client with no issues. My purpose was to determine a mental health rationale for the client's use of marijuana. At the initial assessment, the client indicated use of marijuana since 10-years-of-age and was smoking daily until one month before his assessment. The client admitted to liking marijuana and refers to aspects of marijuana as "nick" and "roach."

The client reported living with mother and an elder brother 14 and visiting with his father once a week. His mother and father are separated and his 18-year old sister lives out of the home. The client admitted at his assessment that he wanted to quit using marijuana, as he wanted his mother to be proud of him, and that he did not want to become an addict. From the reports of both client and mother, the family history indicates no issues with drugs, alcohol or mental health. The client and parent deny any previous treatment of the client for mental health or substance abuse.

Through assessing and counseling the client, he indicates either unawareness or denial as to the serious consequences that may result from using marijuana. The client admits that he could be expelled from school for using marijuana. Nevertheless, he demonstrates the need of learning more about the dangers and consequences of using marijuana.

The client reports his love of playing soccer after school when he arrives home. He also suggests soccer as a substitute for using marijuana. He does not play in a school or city league. Rather he plays with friends in the neighborhood, from whom he probably obtains marijuana. The client claims many friends, but, in his assessment, he claims hanging out with only one. Apparently, the client's circle of friends is limited as well as his interests. However, he is close to his mother and claims that he is also close to his father.

The client demonstrates fluency in spoken English and Spanish and is at least of average to above average intelligence. He was born in the United States and, therefore, grew up in the American education system with ESL classes. His mother, who is also a very pleasant and sweet lady, speaks Spanish fluently, but English very sparsely. The client also speaks of a grandmother and relatives living in the community. The client and mother do not attend church but look to one another for support. Mother also bakes pies for a local food chain and enjoys sharing them with others. She also holds another part time job at night.

Although the psychiatrist reports no mental health issues with the client, I highly suspect that something is going on with him. Perhaps information is yet to be disclosed on the client and family including a mental health diagnosis as well. The client presents as being afraid of school, yet he manages to wake himself up by means of his own alarm clock to attend school. The client indicates eating only one meal per day and indicates not eating more while smoking marijuana. In counseling, I continue wondering about hidden issues and/or diagnoses.

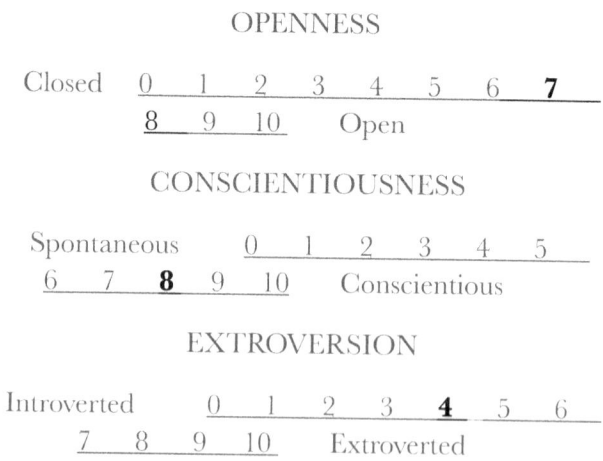

OPENNESS

Closed 0 1 2 3 4 5 6 **7**
        8 9 10   Open

CONSCIENTIOUSNESS

Spontaneous   0 1 2 3 4 5
    6 7 **8** 9 10   Conscientious

EXTROVERSION

Introverted   0 1 2 3 **4** 5 6
        7 8 9 10   Extroverted

Five   Three Personality Sketches

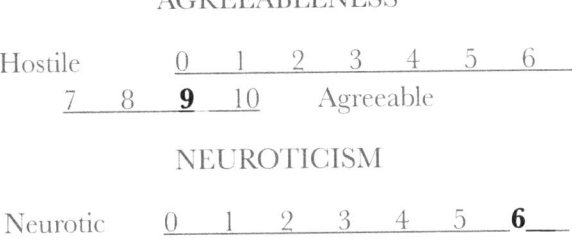

Overall, what stands out with this young man are traits of a pleasant and sweet disposition, his personability. He demonstrates a charismatic attractiveness that makes him easy to accept and believe. He presents as very agreeable; thus he is ranked at 9.5/10 on the continuum of agreeableness. He indicates kindness, warmness, pleasantness, cooperativeness and the like. He indicates openness with his strongest trait of brightness, but other traits are not as conspicuous at this point in his life. Hence, he is ranked with openness at 7/10, which is still 7 intervals from closed.

Of course, his conscientious traits provoke interest since he apparently indicates neatness, steadiness and carefulness, hence, his rank of 8/10. However, his level of extroversion appears low, probably around 4/10, which is four intervals from introversion. Relatively, he indicates traits of neuroticism. For example, his hiddenness indicates insecurity and a lack of trust with probable irritability, nervousness and anxiousness, therefore, ranking the client at 3/10 on the continuum of neuroticism.

The client most likely indicates social anxiety, as he does not gravitate toward larger groups of people.

He admitted this earlier in counseling. His negative dominant traits seem to be indicated with neuroticism, which also include weakness in openness and strength in introversion. In addition, his conscientious traits depict his hiddenness and carefulness.

In addition, the client implicitly demonstrates much internal conflict with others, especially, with adults. He discloses only to a small group or most likely to one peer with whom he will use marijuana. The client maintains a defensive stance even with other peers because they may easily fool and deceive him. Most likely, this client has a deep issue with trust and belongingness. He, in reality, is seeking security and belongingness within himself.

His negatively dominant traits are self-hiddenness, defensiveness, carefulness, neatness, anxiousness and nervousness. He indicates tension with openness over and against closedness, conscientiousness over and against neuroticism, and probable implicit hostility over and against agreeableness. Agreeableness appears as his stronger positive trait over and against hiddenness, as his stronger negative trait. In fact, he indicates hiddenness as the key trait of introversion moving toward the border of hostility.

Though apparently bright, the tone of the client most likely is hidden. He demonstrates unity and harmony in his personality, but in reality, key dominant and subordinate traits are in conflict. The resolution point toward symmetry and balance is that of hiddenness becoming disclosed.

In light of this client's disposition, the question is posed as to why he is using marijuana. In fact, this is his only apparent diagnosis, namely, Cannabis Abuse. What of the relationship between hiddenness and using? Within the client's being and persona is the irritability and stress of tension, which he hides well from many others, peers and adults. However, the stressors of this tension create anxiety in social contexts. Consequently, he enjoys using marijuana because he experiences relaxation as deliverance from irritability and tension continually felt within the self.

Six

Cultural and Artistic Approaches to Counseling

Having considered diagnoses and analyses, I am now moving to the most difficult task of therapy, namely, methods and approaches. However, as with diagnosing and analysis, synthesis and healing also result from self-study and self-analysis. From this, I am expositing counseling approaches and techniques that synergize with the personalities of the three cultural and contextual client personalities group explored in this study.

Person-Centeredness

My first and basic approach with counseling clients is person-centeredness. This begins with the assumption that the counselor presents not as the expert but as mentor and facilitator to the client. The client, in turn, is considered the artist who interreflects with the therapist's knowledge and approach as artist. Also, the therapist who presents as empathic, accepting and congruent is guiding the client into acceptance of self and personality. Essentially, he or she indirectly guides the client to cognizance of potentialities including the social, creative, trustworthy and compassionate. Through interreflecting with the therapist, the client enters into transformative experiences with these potentialities leading to freedom and self-actualization[1]

Therefore, to be effectively person-centered, the counselor must be totally conscious and cognizant of the client's culture so he or she may enter into it. Exercising unconditional positive regard created a context of belongingness and acceptance for the Hispanic American client and his mother. The same is also true of the African-American client and the Anglo-American client.[2]

Empathetic Listening

I listen for cultural nuances and traits that are generally reflected through the family of the client. For example, the Hispanic American client's mother enjoys cooking, and she makes pies, and the client loves his mother's tacos and tortillas. The client loves to play soccer, the football game of his culture. While listening to the client, I encouragingly ask him to share his knowledge and experience of that game. In this manner, his trust is increased and, thereby, congruence. He is empowered with the sense of belonging and home.

The African-American client indicates strong interest and talent playing basketball, and his mother

Six   Cultural and Artistic Approaches to Counseling

is highly invested in this. Nuances relating to his desire and commitment to the game are manifested during the course counseling. In being empathic, counseling involves reflective listening while encouragingly commenting on the sport as the client converses. The client is commended for his hard work as a basketball player, which also interreflects with the African-American Protestant ethic of hard work. The client's trust is increased as well as his sense of belonging and home.

The Anglo-American client, being from an adjacent rural community, finds great interest in hunting and fishing. He also plays several musical instruments and his family is active in an evangelical church setting. Listening reflectively to him and his parents, leads to questions and responses about the client's interests, church activities and even his father's work. The father highly values his work as a water works administrator for the city. He had also worked in sewers in the past. Through counseling, I have been able to build empathy, congruence and a strong sense of belongingness on the part the client and his parents. We interreflected with their strong middle class ethos of hard work, family and the out-of-doors.

Tactful Questioning

Another phase of counseling includes questioning the client but not interrogatively. Asking questions is applied in the context of reflective listening. Open ended and closed ended questions may be applied. In essence, questions are presented tactfully while taking into consideration the needs

91

and sensitivities of the client. In counseling, listening is fundamentally the imperative for constructive and sensitive questioning. Effort is applied from making the client feel as if I am intrusive and badgering. Often questions are presented in the context of reflective comments and conversations. Essentially, the goal of questioning is to learn and enter into the client's story, namely, the life story and autobiography.

The Autobiography

As indicated earlier, the autobiography interreflects with the worldviews and personalities of clients. The more learned about clients, the more I enter into the worldviews and personalities of clients. My ability to assess personality deficits and sufficits is increased. Through applying empathy, congruency and belongingness, I enter into a relaxed relationship with clients conveying moments of friendship and kindness. Clients find greater ease in reciprocating with greater openness and trust.

They experience a greater sense of belonging in the counseling relationship than previously. By stating the adverb previously, I mean that clients, who first enter the counseling and assessing process, may feel somewhat skeptical, distant and estranged. Such emotions become my greatest challenge when meeting clients face-to-face for the first time.

When first meeting with the Hispanic American client and his mother, they presented as very pleasant people. This client entered counseling through another

Six   Cultural and Artistic Approaches to Counseling

assessing therapist. At our first counseling session, I gathered information on the client's personality traits from his diagnostic and treatment history. After four weeks into the counseling relationship, I learned that the client tends to hold back information. Of course, with mother lacking total fluency in English and the counselor lacking fluency in Spanish, we are unable to discuss the client's story effectively. However, she felt relaxed enough in the counseling relationship to offer to bake me a pie.

In fact, she and her son represent a culture of hospitality. From their purview, sharing cooking provides the way of showing appreciation and increasing relationships. Of course, turning down the offer may have offended mother and client so I accepted it. Later I shared the pie with other colleagues. I also informed my supervisors about this. Nevertheless, I understand this custom because I also grew up in the same culture of hospitality. Overall, hospitality relative to counseling means making one feel at home in that relationship. This is the sense of belonging that I am working toward.

Parental Involvement

Within four weeks, I was able to grasp enough characteristics of the client to express his story and therefrom sufficits and deficits of his personality. As with an initial piano student, much of the time over the first several lessons is spent creating an atmosphere of acceptance and belonging with the student and his or her parent. I also require parents to be involved in piano lessons as this invests the parent totally into the learning experiences of the student. This approach to piano pedagogy is borrowed from the Suzuki music education method, which finds its origins in Japan. Historically, Japanese education has always been both parent and student centered.[3]

My approach to counseling involves the parent with the client in sessions. Counseling focused upon client and parent leads the parent to total investment in the client's counseling development. Nevertheless, periods arise calling for the need of single sessions involving only the client and only the parent. Effective involvement in contextual and cultural therapy includes listening to parent and client as they talk about themselves, the family and the client. As a result, I am able to enter into the client's story and life.

Belongingness

This is very true not only with my Hispanic client, but my Caucasian and African-American clients. Progress through the weeks of sessions has led to an effective counseling relationship of belonging. All three clients and their parents apparently demonstrate no problems with answering questions, sharing information and even donating urine specimens for drug testing. On a Likert scale of 0 to 10, trust in the therapist has increased on average from ~04/10 to ~09/10. On this scale of trust, 0 indicates absolutely no trust and 10 indicates absolutely total trust. Overall, trust means that the client is open

Six   Cultural and Artistic Approaches to Counseling

and comfortable with the therapist in that he feels safe enough in the counseling relationship to share information that is very personal and sensitive.

Openness and Collaboration

Once clients, like my piano students, feel at home, namely, in the place of safety, belonging, trust and openness, counseling reaches another level. This is the point of acceptance and readiness for openness and collaboration. In this context, therapist and client freely interact regarding the clients' strengths and weaknesses (sufficits and deficits). Clients freely share their stories centered on the topic of the session. As I listen and observe, I maintain a smile of acceptance so that when I give them feedback, we effectively discuss deficits in the context of sufficits.

As we focus on the modification of deficits, I seek to convey their potential, as if it is present yet progressing into the future. Clients of adolescent and young adulthood often see the present rather than the future. Hence, counseling must be present active because potential and future are definite realities. Clients are encouraged to set short goals rather than long-term goals that the *telos* or ultimate purpose may be achieved.

As with piano students who also have reached safety, security and belonging, we ourselves openly discuss technic in terms of sufficits and deficits. With adolescents and children, my approach with teaching is present tense while treating future potential in present tense understanding. Small goals of technic development are set and reached with the implicit future purpose and *telos* of artistry.

As with piano students, I listen to clients. I observe their behaviors and expressions. I ask questions that I may experience their life stories, but in the initial stages of relating to them, I often hear partial stories, which at times are bits and pieces of the total life story. Yet these stories are easiest for them to tell in that they feel more comfortable with them. The same is true of piano students, who feel at home playing short melodies and exercises until they reach the comfort level of playing whole compositions.

Waiting and Patience

Counseling is a slow process involving waiting and working with clients over time. Thorough counseling involves patience with clients. Clients must be permitted to grow in the safety and comfort of the counseling relationship. Demonstrating compassion and patience leads clients to an enhanced awareness of personality traits as reflected in their stories. In essence, learning their stories as a therapist is equivalent to mastering a complex sonata of one of the great masters such as Beethoven. Through therapy, the mastery and knowledge of personalities is attained through reflective listening, observing, and tactful questioning. Such techniques permit entrance into the intricacies of depth and hiddenness existing between pieces of the story. As a pianist, I seek to master intricacies of phrases and nuances so that I

Six   Cultural and Artistic Approaches to Counseling

may ultimately bring them together into the whole.

Mentoring and Empowering

As with piano students, who become invested in identity with the instrument, I mentor clients into becoming invested with their personalities. Guiding them through eliciting pieces of their story, leads them to increased awareness of the life and power of their story. Through eliciting, reflective listening, and tactfully questioning clients, they share with me and learn much about themselves. Eventually they become empowered through the living compositions of their life stories.

During this process though, I am careful with guiding clients into becoming what I want them to become. As clients become, they must form their identities apart from mine. This is very difficult in that such a process is implicitly deceptive. I may be assured of leading clients to take charge of their personalities, yet, in reality, they are being disempowered from self-control, self-management and self-directedness. Even if the goal that I conceive for them is great and noble, such a *telos* is not worthy of them. Instead I must be fully aware that I am guiding them collaboratively, openly and carefully to arrive at their *telos*.

As with clients' stories, the artist's story must be his or her own which includes its substance, its structure and its *telos*. The painting, drawing or sculpture must belong to the artist. The poem, essay, novel or music composition must belong to the artist. The story must have its own beginning, middle and end. It must have its own theme, premise and/or thesis. It must have its own tone, meter and rhythm.

As the artist who reaches into the depth of self and personality so clients must reach into the depths of self and personality. Ultimately they reach the empowerment to create a self, personality and worldview that is maturing with the beauty of symmetry and balance through self-actualization. Devising the key theme of a work of art involves reaching down into the depths of self and personality and pulling it up. Such a task requires much self-reflection, and clients alone may do this. The therapist cannot. Nevertheless, therapy involves motivating and encouraging clients through reflective listening, patience, compassion and tactful questioning with the ultimate end of clients becoming the creators of their lives and personalities.

In this way, clients are empowered to paint and repaint their stories. As artists, clients shape and reshape a composition, the personality and reflective story until mastered. Clients work toward a masterpiece, which is depicted in the personality's moving to maturity and self-actualization. However, unlike the final painting, sculpture, music composition, poem, essay or novel, the personality is ever maturing. This maturing unto maturing is the *telos* denoted by self-actualization. The self, as personality, reaches the uniqueness and beauty of self, persona and worldview. This is the completed composition of the artist, which in the sense of the concert performance of a masterpiece is never really final but always processually maturing.

Six   Cultural and Artistic Approaches to Counseling

Nevertheless, as clients reach readiness and teachability, they are guided collaboratively into a greater knowledge of personality deficits and sufficits than most likely already known. Readiness refers to clients' trust levels as increasing to the point of comfortably entering into a therapeutic critique, which collaboratively takes place in the context of sufficits. Also, critiquing involves totally interrelating with the client regarding deficits while teachability refers to guiding the client into the *why* and *how* of deficits. Resultantly, the client becomes receptive to working with solutions that either translate deficits into sufficits and/or replacing deficits with sufficits. For example, as the artist works to achieve effective tone quality with changing forms, lines and/or colors and their gradations from deepest dark to highest light/white, so the client is guided into shaping and reshaping the deficits and sufficits of personality.

Spirituality and Creativity

Spirituality underscores much of multicultural counseling. In my autobiography, religion and spirituality have played an important part in my culture, life and development. Religion and spirituality have been the life of my worldview. Religion and spirituality also play themselves out in counseling clients. Spirituality provides the heart of religion. It is the vital source while religion is the form. Spirituality cannot totally be separated from a client's religion, but principles of spirituality may be extracted and practiced by those outside of particular religious contexts. In fact, many universal principles of spirituality have been defined, but I will not expound upon them here; nevertheless, they will be suggested in this discussion.

All in all, much discussed in this study involves spirituality, for example, unconditional positive regard of the other, giving the other a sense of belongingness and home, often called hospitality, and being patient and waiting on the other. All of these principles are summed up in the love of God and neighbor as you would the self. As for the certainty of a Higher Power, this differs in varied religions. In some religious schools, Higher Power is presented as metabeing or force, and in others, the concept is presented as divine person, namely God, Christ, Holy Spirit, or Great Spirit.

In counseling contexts, my clients have come from either Protestant or Catholic backgrounds. For them God is a living person, infinite and omnipotent. Christ is conveyed as God in the flesh and the Savior from sin, death and disease. In more liberal Protestant groups, skepticism exists as to the divinity of Christ and as to the traditional orthodox definition of the Holy Trinity, as being One God, yet Father, Son and Holy Spirit.

However, many of the young people in counseling have not defined their religious, spiritual beliefs and values and are either dependent upon their parents for spirituality, or they are questioning belief in a supreme being. Hence, out of genuine positive regard for them, I major in the culture while applying spiritual principles in my approaches

Six   *Cultural and Artistic Approaches to Counseling*

of counseling. If a client asks about religion and spirituality, I respond with caution but will do my best to answer questions.

Although, I am an Eastern Orthodox priest, I am not counseling in the context of that Faith. Rather I am counseling the public in a grant-funded, private, community agency. The latter therefore provides the paradigm for conveying spirituality in counseling. A strong non-partial Eastern Orthodox spiritual principle that I work with and strive to relate to others in counseling is that of faith and prayer of the heart. I strive to guide clients into deep self-reflection and mindfulness of their thoughts and emotions. To move deeply into self is to touch the heart, the seat of being, and therein clients may join thoughts with emotions.

At this point, they will move toward self-mastery. Eastern Orthodox monks pray the prayer of Jesus continually in their hearts, but prayer of the heart does not always involve the Jesus prayer, "Lord Jesus Christ, Son of God, have mercy on me a sinner." Rather a spiritual phrase from the Bible or other sources may be repeated and meditated upon as affirmation for the soul. Lay people in Eastern Orthodoxy most likely takes this latter approach.

Meditation and prayer is a universal spiritual practice and is effective through learning mindfulness[4] or in the Greek Orthodox sense, *Nepsis*.[5] This involves constant vigilance of the flow of thoughts and emotions within the mind and heart. Awareness of these thoughts and emotions indicates mindfulness.

The end of mindfulness meditation is the realization that thoughts and emotions are harmless and that they can only impact on you as much as they are allowed. Also, this *terminus* involves freeing the mind of their influence so that you may move on with life. Negative thoughts need be separated from positive thoughts while embracing positive thoughts and emotions that are true through affirmations that empower us.

At the same time, spirituality is manifested in creativity. In fact, the book of Genesis(1:1) opens with the verse: "In the beginning God created ..." The positive acts of man image the creation of God. These acts demonstrate love for God, neighbor, brother and the creation. In this study, the end of counseling is creativity, the creation of self. Creativity includes acts of healing, which are, in turn, demonstrated through acts of loving-kindness (*mitzvah*).[6] When the self is creatively transformed, than others are transformed. Creativity is the greatest gift of God to humankind. Creativity displays the image of God in the heart. The artist, through the centuries has displayed the gift of creativity to the world. As art and creativity are acts of the heart synergized with mind, so true faith and spirituality are acts of the heart synergized with mind.

In this study, effective counseling conveys the synergism of mind and heart, the affective and cognitive domains of the psyche. As counseling reaches into these domains in clients than the multifaceted person of the client is effectively treated. This is the essential act of spirituality in counseling, namely, to bridge cognitive and affective domains

Six   Cultural and Artistic Approaches to Counseling

while igniting the creative act of the psyche. One need not be labeled an artist to be creative and a minister or priest to be spiritual. These two qualities image the divine in every person.

Concomitantly, as the self finds harmony through the synergism of cognitive and affective domains, counseling also facilitates the synergism of self with the other. A strong assumption derived from Genesis 1:1 is that the language of creativity results in the creation. In the English language, the concepts create, creation, and creativity are expressed by the same root, create. The ultimate creative act of union of mind and heart engenders unity with the creation, namely, human, animal, vegetable, and mineral and the elements of earth, fire, water and air. The end of counseling as creativity involves the composition of self that is in harmony, symmetry and balance with personality and being. Such a person is at one with self and world. Such a person has reached self-mastery and all nature and being have entered with self and psyche completing a living composition of being, self and psyche.

Seven

Counseling and Personality Portraiture
An Anglo-American Approach

As stated above, Anglo-American client is indicated with deficits related to social anxiety and introversion. Relatively, we noted in him extreme sensitivity to his parents, especially, his father. Reflectively, the client most likely is insecure and defensive around most adults. The client seems to gravitate toward positive activities of music performance, hunting and fishing, that is, activities that moreso involve the self rather than others. In all probability, one approach that I take is suggesting (not telling) that he begin gradually involving one or even two others in his ventures. This may easily be accomplished with fishing and hunting. However, with music performance, he most likely engages in practice sessions with at least one other peer, especially, with playing a brass or woodwind instrument. My overarching goal through counseling is guiding the client into finding greater harmony and balance in life, which translates to his worldview and personality. Guiding the client through collaboration to increased inroads stimulating greater extraverted involvements will generate greater balance and harmony in his life and personality.

Other artistic approaches through counseling conveyed to the client are those of rhythm and tone. Since this client is a music student, talking with him in this manner is beneficial. In music, rhythm is its heartbeat. Rhythm is the pace of life and is generally steady and vibrant. However, even miscounting musical beats and even misinterpreting and/or misreading sections of a composition may interrupt the pace of its rhythm. The client's deficits of social anxiety and introversion most likely interrupt his life rhythm and, therefore, the tone of his pleasant disposition. Hence, the client is encouraged to be mindful of the rhythm of breathing through change of dispositions from tones of pleasantness to tones of fear and anxiety. As the client becomes cognizant of breathing, he will strive to maintain its same rhythmic pace through pleasantness and anxiety. Once accomplished, he will experience empowerment over anxiety. Also, being mindful of thoughts and feelings through all mood changes will eventually permit the transfer of positive thoughts and feelings substantiating pleasantness to states of worry and introversion. The client will eventually modify anxiety and introversion.

Thoughts and feelings provide the ideas and thematic material for tones of disposition. Enabling the client to become aware of thoughts and feelings requires teaching him about this. He has to become cognizant of the life of thoughts and feelings inside of his being and their power to drive his life. If he does not manage them, they may mismanage his being and personality especially through social anxiety and introversion. Reflectively, he must become aware that he is the artist who is to design and manage the composition of his life and worldview.

As in a painting, tone and thematic material is strongly conveyed by color, line and shape with gradations of color from deepest dark to highest light or white. This also is true with tone color regarding harmony and melody, the substance of thematic material in music. Guiding the client with the idea of playing his musical instruments when he feels anxious or stressed should also help him to rechannel his thinking from low tones of anxiety to high tones of pleasantness, creativity and vigor. Encouraging the client to use music is giving him control over the color gradations of his life and is helping him to substantiate a harmoniously, varied and colorful worldview. As the client learns by applying this approach consistently, he will become empowered as the artist of his life.

Also, the client's love of the out-of-doors is of advantage to him. Especially, when experiencing worry, social anxiety and introverted aloneness, the client, as did Beethoven, may immerse himself into the living and vibrant experiences of the out-of-doors. Observing the color contrasts of terrain and the rhythmic flow of streams and rivers as well as seeing, hearing and feeling the wind rushing through tree tops may move the client from worry to stability. He may also experience the life of the out-of-doors giving him a sense of freedom and wellbeing. Taking advantage of nature is reinvigorating and most likely will stimulate the client's creative energy.

Together, as we collaborate in counseling sessions on these experiences undertaken by the client, we experience his empowerment as the artist and manager of his life. He develops power to see into the depths of his mind and personality and to recreate his personality and worldview into a "world" free of traits related to anxiety and introversion. At the same time, his tendencies to these will always be somewhere in the picture, but they do not have to be the key themes of his life and being.

Outcomes of counseling experienced by Anglo-American client and myself are determined as follows. The client seems relaxed with the therapist in the counseling context. He is demonstrating very little if any tension during interactions. He has reached the place where he is now motivated for self-exploration and is taking on and making new attempts to achieve artistry with his life and personality. He is open and appears accepting of the process of reflective listening. All in all, the client demonstrates the experience of acceptance, congruity and belongingness in the counseling relationship. Apparently, he is moving toward his meaning for being and realizing the transformation of self-actualization.

Overall, the *raison d'etre* of the client, his reason for being, is to lead him into finding meaning and purpose for existence. The client, as artist, is finding this meaning in the power experienced through finding joy and fulfillment in creating the composition of his personality. As illustrated, teaching him to apply the elements of music and art to his life and personality strengthens his sufficits and modifies his deficits. Resultantly, he is given charge over life and self as he experiences the power of developing, shaping and recreating the substance and structure of his personality.

An African-American Approach

Unlike the above client, we have noticed the African-American client as living and breathing in another cultural and family life. We have already noted this client as born and reared in a low-income home of poverty. Unlike his Anglo-American counterpart, he has faced education, economic, social and family limitations beginning in his home of rearing by his mother and maternal grandmother. He does not know his father; therefore, the familial male role model has not been present for him to mime. However, his ability to play basketball has given him a basketball coach at school to supply that male role model for him. This is the positive experience in this boy's life, unlike many other peers, from the same race and ethnicity, who find themselves facing the criminal justice system as their male role model.

In counseling with this client, my intention is, of course, to draw upon this Client's positive experiences and talents as an athlete and basketball player. In fact, he is not merely a basketball player but a basketball star in high school. His coach and school appear to have much invested in this young man because he is winning games for them. In working with this client and his mother, while receiving reports from his sessions with the psychiatrist, I have learned that much is being placed on this client not only by his school but his family. As stated above, his mother and family, as the way out of poverty, look to him. Evidently, this client's worldview is summed up in the thematic material of basketball playing and the theme of basketball star. Everything else seems secondary and even tertiary in this client's purview.

We also noted that this client's personality demonstrates traits of being outgoing and gregarious, yet stressors related to Depressive Disorder NOS and ADHD-Combined Type are opposing such personality traits. Although these stressors pull down on the client's positive personality traits, counseling supports the client's ability to compensate with his high motivation to achieve in the basketball arena. The client already has created a composition of self as the key theme or, if you will, the key metaphor, the star basketball player. He presents as handsome, 5'10" in height and slim, yet muscular. He is well liked and popular at school. Over the years, he molded himself into this center of interest. Nevertheless, as his therapist, my concerns have to do primarily with basketball as his sole world and the self-medication of his depression and ADHD with marijuana. On the positive side, his involvement with basketball also compensates for his deficits.

Through counseling, the client is guided to take charge over these negative traits so that he may strengthen tones of brightness and personableness in the face of tendencies toward anger, irritability and sadness. Like the artist, I, as counselor, am teaching the client to maintain the positive colors, shapes and forms of his worldview as well as the pleasingly strong tones that they convey. He has shaped the balance and harmony of the composition of his life and worldview since childhood. Nevertheless, I am attempting to guide him into seeing the possibility and even the probability of contrasts in his composition. Due to his obsession with self as basketball star, he most likely is pushing contrasts to the side or bottom of his canvas, therefore, displaying imbalance and disproportion.

My aim is to guide him, yes, not only into maintaining the strength of his worldview, but to add contrasts that will enrich his canvas. By guiding him through questions and facilitating his posing of questions, he is becoming aware of other needs, interests and possibilities. Suggestions are given regarding the need to elevate his grades, the need to develop a realistic picture of self after high school, the need of developing deeper relationships with a few friends, and the need of finding another hobby or outlet.

From my vantage point, I can relate to the client. As a boy, I desired to become a concert pianist beginning in junior high school on through college. My worldview comprised of self as concert pianist, and everyone who knew me shared my vision. However, over the years, I have had to work and develop contrasts within the frame of my worldview even to the point of transforming secondary and tertiary interests that were pushed to the sides and bottom of my canvas into truly helpful supports for a transformative definition of self.

In returning to the client's emotional concerns along with his tendency to self-medicate, I referred him to our psychiatrist who has been working with his issues. He is counseling with him and prescribing medication for his disorders, but the client still continues to use marijuana. Most likely, the client is somewhat unsatisfied deep within his being. Most likely, he is fighting with the abrasiveness of not only his emotional and psychological shortcomings but also the stress of having to maintain his stance, namely, to remain the star.

I have encouraged him not to use marijuana by drug testing him as ordered by the school, but this has been to no avail. In fact, I do not truly believe that drug testing is the answer for this client. In reality, this disempowers him from taking charge over his life, namely, empowering him as the artist of his composition of life. Relatively, I have come to the conclusion that strengthening his worldview and developing balanced contrasts is ultimately the way to sobriety. Of course, he has also received education relative to the dangers and disadvantages of using marijuana, other drugs and alcohol.

Strengthening this client's worldview with balanced contrasts should enhance his meaning in life, his *raison d'etre*. As noted, he finds meaning and purpose in himself as a basketball star and player.

Seven — Counseling and Personality Portraiture

The shapes, forms and colors define and enhance the client as star. Again the client has spent years being the artist that has designed this canvas of self in his arena, yet that meaning will be enhanced for him once he learns to expand positive contrasts that enhance the self as star in the arena. In this way the client will begin to create a canvas of comparison-contrast rather than one of contrasts as oppositions being pushed off to the side so as to avoid conflict, imbalance and fragmentation in his personality and worldview.

Client outcomes in counseling, overall, define his experience and progress level in the counseling relationship. This client demonstrated a sense of belongingness in that he felt at home in the relationship. He demonstrated a head start in designing a self and personality of meaning and purposefulness. Recently, he conveys that he has learned the value of carrying on his control as artist, but is somewhat apprehensive about continuing in the development of his portrait and composition of self.

This client is reluctant to give up marijuana and is most likely continuing to struggle with increasing contrasts in his portraiture. Perhaps he is obsessed with clinging to himself as basketball star even to the exclusion of all else for fear of losing his dream of self. Perhaps in time, as the client continues in counseling, he will feel secure enough to increase background and contrasts to the point of even enriching his theme of self as center of interest.

An Hispanic American Approach

Next, we are considering the Hispanic American client who is the youngest of the above two clients. Being 13, he does not share the maturity of his 18-year-old African-American and 15-year-old Anglo-American counterparts. He displays a great difference in the way he responds to counseling in comparison to the other clients. This client is slowly responding to the need of becoming self-directed as an artist. He also is taking more time in responding to my interactions with him. However, he is pleasant and friendly as we noted above. He is struggling with becoming more accepting of counseling.

The client, although born in the United States, has to face acculturation problems, which may be impacting on his life, personality and school performance. The family income is low, and father and mother are separated. Mother appears to be sole provider for the client and his elder brother 14. The client also claims that he has an elder sister 18 living in Mexico with the mother's family. As we noted, mother is a very pleasant and sweet lady who speaks very little English. She and the client speak in Spanish with one another while the client speaks in English with me, especially during therapy sessions.

Above we also noted that the client appears to be hiding many of his feelings and thoughts. At the same time, he maintains a friendly stance. When trying to find out from the client why he will yield clean drug tests and then relapse on his last drug test, he has trouble responding. He is aware that he must yield a negative drug screen for his last test in order to complete the Level I Substance Abuse program.

In addition, he claims that he and friends will play soccer in the neighborhood. Then he will say that his mother will not let him go out and play. He also reported that he got in trouble at school for kissing a girl and denied knowing the unacceptability of this action until he was sent to the office. The therapist could not help but chuckle.

Apparently, the client is fishing for answers and his answers indicate broken thoughts. He has not formed a cohesive identity at this point in life. He presents as incoherent. Most likely, he is unable to find connections between thoughts, ideas and sentences. When I asked about grades in school, he demonstrated trouble in sharing information regarding his applied work. However, he indicated earning 64% on one academic paper and that his GPA was low.

The client displays age-appropriate immaturity, but also is unable to demonstrate unity, coherence and emphasis in thinking and speaking. He speaks English well, but has not learned to connect his speaking with writing and other facets of self. He is very close to his mother and father but also "hangs out" with a small group of Hispanic boys in the neighborhood. He is also close to his maternal and paternal relatives and cousins in the community.

His apparent hiddenness may indicate an acculturation problem because the client may be having trouble integrating with the mainstream culture at school.[1] He is aware that I am not Hispanic and undoubtedly feels insecure in sharing information with me. The psychiatrist found no mental health diagnoses in the client, and this may or may not be possible. Nevertheless, the client most likely demonstrates a low trust level for the mainstream, which is by nature middle class Anglo-American. Of no help to the client is his low socioeconomic level, which also increases his fear and insecurity with self relative to Anglo-American culture.

I am now led to the question as to why the client smokes marijuana? Why does he abstain for a short period and then relapse? Through interactions with him, I am postulating that using marijuana is his way of identifying with his small neighborhood peer group. He does no share information on his source for marijuana, but he does say: he will "find it at the bus stop." He denies receiving it from anyone there.

The client may find solace in marijuana because of the stress and strain of being alone and lost in a predominantly middle-class Anglo-American culture. The client is caught in the middle of tension between being agreeable and conscientious yet Introverted and neurotic. As we said, he is most likely hidden, irritable, nervous and anxious. These are certainly traits of struggling with acculturation by trying to integrate and not being able to do so. Thus the client will identify with his own group in his lower socio-economic Hispanic neighborhood.

This therapist has observed and experienced many of these traits regarding the tension of acculturation reflecting culture shock. My experience with culture shock reaches back to my seminary days as a 26-year-old having never been out of my small country town of Anglo-American cultural background. In a few hours' time by plane, I landed in New York City to study for the Eastern Orthodox priesthood in a Russian Orthodox Seminary. This small school was made up of faculty and students from all over the United States, Canada, Western and Eastern Europe, the Middle East and the Far East. Two or three of us of Anglo-American cultural persuasion were struggling with a wide array of foreign cultures. I felt empty, lost and alone and was nervous, anxious, and irritable. I felt as if I was wrapped smothering in a cocoon. Through much difficulty in forming relationships, I became introverted.

With this understanding, I am striving to build an empathic relationship of acceptance and congruity with this client and his mother. I am striving to listen to him reflectively and to ask tactful questions with the attempt to elicit answers and questions from him. So far, I have received very few questions from him. He is very polite, kind and pleasant with me. He will say yes sir and no sir. He will even say thank you and no thank you.

I continue to be patient waiting for him to experience belongingness and a sense of being at home in the counseling relationship. I sense that he is struggling to understand our relationship as he is referred to counseling not by his own choice but through the duress of his school, drug policy. This along with drug testing does not facilitate the client's trust or belonging in the counseling relationship. At the same time, enforced drug testing is not teaching the client the self-trust needed for self-direction to become the artist of his own composition of personality and worldview.

In the counseling relationship, much time is given to increase the strength and power of our relationship while gradually guiding him into the harmony of personality and worldview. Through increasing our discussions we are delving deeply into his interests and strengths. These include his love of soccer and his love of father, mother and family. Perhaps he will eventually sense the need to share information regarding his neighborhood, peer group. Through this process, his strengths of agreeableness and conscientiousness as well as apparent openness will be affirmed. Also, we will discuss his acculturation issues, and, possibly make connections with aspects of Anglo-American culture that he may possibly like and be curious about.

Right now, the thesis of his personality includes pleasantness and apparent personableness. At this point, his personality does not demonstrate a substantial purpose or interest other than the possibility of playing soccer at school or the community. Presently, the client plays soccer in the neighborhood. Unlike the African-American client or Anglo-American client of this study, he has not begun to consider purposefulness and other substantial interests.

Seven — Counseling and Personality Portraiture

The client's worldview is comprised of the thesis of self as sweet, pleasant and friendly. In his supporting background, he indicates his mother and father who are separated and his relatives. He also speaks of playing soccer and smoking marijuana with a small peer group. In the outermost circle of his worldview exists the Anglo-American world from which he isolates himself.

In leading the client as artist to recreate his own composition, he will develop it in a Hispanic cultural backdrop. He will maintain his dominant traits and thesis of a pleasant and friendly self with a sweet disposition. Other subdominant traits will be his family, friends and relatives. At the same time, he will be guided into an increased interest in soccer, perhaps, even playing soccer in school or in the community. This can become his identity and his *raison d'etre*. Also, he will be guided into connecting with aspects of the Anglo-American world that he would even be remotely interested in or open to. In this way, the client is composing a thematic essay of dominance and contrast with variations and repetition. This will formulate as he is guided into increasing his friendships, increasing his interests, and connecting gradually with the Anglo-American cultural worldview.

Currently, this client has not found harmony and balance, but rather is caught with a worldview and personality of imbalance and disproportion. His composition demonstrates brightness of personal disposition, but much of who he is remains hidden. His composition does not demonstrate comparison-contrast with variation but is limited in ideas, purposefulness and meaningfulness. Although bright, his personality is flat. Although extraverted, it is hidden. Although open, it is closed. Much of the client's personality remains hidden and undeveloped due to immaturity and issues with acculturation.

    In essence, a wall exists between who this client is and isn't. This wall hinders many positive and effective counseling outcomes. Counseling may not effect positive development with the hidden. This client, unlike the others, is still in the very early stages of acceptance and congruity. On a Likert scale of 0 to 10, with 0 meaning not at all accepting and congruent and 10 meaning totally accepting and congruent, this client appears to be on a level of 4/10 at the lowest and 6/10 at the highest. This is the reason that counseling for this client will involve patience and waiting while striving to reflectively listen to and exchange questions and answers.

Seven   Counseling and Personality Portraiture

Eight

Assumptions and Conclusion

Throughout my tenure of twenty-five years as a professional counselor and therapist, I have continually served the same student aged population that I have served at Insight Human Services. Overall, I estimate that I have counseled with at least 6000 Clients and their families, the majority of which have been boys. At my current agency for the past ten years, I have most likely counseled with approximately 1000 clients and their families. Prior to writing this piece, I have perused 700 profiles of my student population at Insight. I have considered these in the light of my multicultural male population over my total years of counseling. Also, I have even looked back at the youth that I have served as a teacher as well as a pastor. From these, I was able to choose the profiles of three key young people that most likely typify the personality traits of the composite cultural groups whom I have served. At the same time, these profiles convey my overall approaches and methodologies of counseling applied over the years. Herein, I have related to these counseling approaches as personality counseling portraiture. As I have said, I am mentoring clients into becoming artists composing the portraits of their unique personalities.

Thus, the reader has noted this piece as not a scientific treatise posing hypotheses with the attempt to quantifiably or even qualifiedly prove or disprove them. This study is not presented as a scholarly thesis demonstrating my attempt to expound a unique thesis with the necessary corroborations that would satisfy the academicians of the counseling world. Rather the reader most likely noted its content as autobiographical. My self as a counselor is conveyed from eclectic experiences in diverse cultural and spiritual contexts while exercising gifts and talents of the fine arts. Concomitantly, throughout my student and adult life, I have acquired a strong humanities and social sciences education, and have been extensively involved not only in counseling, but in teaching and the ordained ministry. Nevertheless, the major emphasis of my professional adult life has been in the occupation of counseling youth and families.

As indicated, I look at my self as artist and philosopher and my work of counseling as an art. Thus from my viewpoint as an educator, I see myself mentoring clients. Earlier, I spoke of the pedagogue model, which is not merely to instruct but to nurture and guide the multifaceted person of the psyche. Counseling, therefore, guides, nurtures and facilitates the learning and self-actualization of the client personality. As indicated herein, personality is not static but dynamic. Personality is pliable and moldable and must be composed and recomposed

Seven   Counseling and Personality Portraiture

by the self of the client. Personality is likened to a musical composition, a written treatise or poem and even a painting such as a scene or portrait. The therapist as pedagogue mentors the client into self-actualization, namely, into becoming a unique and completing person. Such a person demonstrates the uniqueness of individuation of personality whose traits are wholly synthesized and balanced. This is the final masterpiece of the artist-counselor.

Like the artist, I, as counselor, must consider my materials and media. Of course, these include clients of cultural and spiritual diversity. The cultural milieu and family contexts of clients provide the material and means of molding them. I spoke of the uniqueness of many cultures, especially, those making up Anglo-American, African-American and Hispanic American clients. Being a Lebanese American, reared in an immigrant context, has allowed my connections with the uniqueness of other cultures as is the case of counseling clients from the three aforementioned cultures. I have counseled clients from other cultures as well, but these three cultures have provided the majority of my clients.

Counseling multicultural personalities meets the challenges of acculturation into Anglo-American life. This latter culture, of course, is the predominant one in the United States, especially, the middling class dimension of this culture. We noted the unique struggles of African-American and Hispanic youth and their families in adapting to a way that is foreign to them. We also, looked at the problem of assimilation, which traditionally in Anglo-American culture has demanded that foreign nationals lose the uniqueness of cultural and ethnic identity for the sake of "blending in" with the predominant culture. However, the darker the skin color of a people, the more difficult such a people will have "blending in" to the predominant culture, which is white or very fair in skin color. Hence, the first generations of third world countries along with their descendants must intermarry with the White middle-class race as well as learn the latter's customs and traditions.

The challenge of the counselor as artist, thusly, is to facilitate the acculturation of ethnic groups, especially those of third world origin. Blacks, although growing up in the United States, still live under the impact of the antebellum South and the succeeding era of Jim Crow. At the same time, the majority of Hispanics immigrating to the United States also struggle with learning a new language, customs and traditions of Anglo-American middle-class culture. Conversely, the latter group must learn to acculturate with African-Americans and Hispanics, and, in turn, these latter two groups must learn to acculturate with one another.

The fundamental end of acculturation is adaptability. This definitely does not involve assimilation. Rather adaptability results through syncretism. In reality, all cultures are empowered when its peoples learn one another's language and tradition. Adaptability is also facilitated when cultures of peoples adapt to or truly learn one another's customs and mannerisms. This would include understanding beliefs and values, philosophies, religions and spiritualties. Thus, the fundamental end of multicultural counseling is to facilitate adaptability for ethnic and even Anglo-American clients. True adaptability with syncretism is engendered not only with multicultural education but also with fostering in clients a strong sense of relational belonging with others of cultural diversity.

Relative to the artistic end of counseling includes not only cultural adaptability but spirituality. Spirituality through counseling with all positive traits of the counselor's personality portrait and autobiography is conveyed to the client. Yet, at the same time, underling one's spiritual personality are those of self-direction and self-reflection. Self-reflection begins with counseling and ends with counseling, and counseling concludes with positive and effective client self-direction. The developing of spirituality of the client personality involves the self-reflection of one's autobiography and inner being. This includes becoming aware of weaknesses and strengths, talents, abilities and needs as opposed to desires. In this way, the counselor is able to guide the client in this same self-awareness, and, as the client increases in self-awareness, the self develops a greater awareness of other and world. Social awareness than translates into positive social skills. Through the counseling process, the client is guided through an understanding of the positive value of self and other and may inquire and accept Being above being,

Overall, my goal for counseling, as suggested in this self-study, is to lead clients to self-transformation and self-direction. This is the therapeutic end of counseling as suggested by the Greek concept, *therapeuo*.[1] Concomitantly, I see self-direction as an apt description of the metaphor, the client as artist. The client is guided to develop the creative self-awareness through guided self-reflection. In turn, this facilitates, the client's creative and effective development and composition of the personality portrait of self.

Fini

Eight Assumptions and Conclusion

Notes

Chapter One

1   Counselling and Self-awareness, http://www.thecounsellorsguide.co.uk/counselling-self-awareness.html (accessed September 21, 2013); Ahmed, Shamshad et al., What Does It Mean to Be a Culturally-Competent Counselor? *The Special Issue on Multicultural Social Justice Leadership Development*, Guest Editor: Carlos P. Zalaquett, University of South Florida; http://www.psysr.org/jsacp/ahmed-v3n1-11_17-28.pdf (accessed September 21, 2013).

2   Kfeir, http://kfeir.com (accessed November 25, 2014).; http://www.kfeir.com/village.html (accessed November 25, 2014).; http://en.wikipedia.org/wiki/Kfeir (accessed November 25, 2014);

3   Leon and Olga Conus, http://www.amazon.com/Fundamentals-Piano-Technique-Olga-Conus/product-reviews/0874876605 (accessed on September 30, 2014); Olga Conus, http://homepages.uwp.edu/mckeever/MadameConusArticle.html (accessed on September 30, 2014).

4   In considering Philippians 3:12-13, I am focusing on the Greek concept, *katalambano*, meaning to lay hold on, namely, to seize and to apprehend, http://biblehub.com/greek/2638.htm

5   Unconditional Positive Regard with Genuineness, http://www.psychologytoday.com/blog/what-doesnt-kill-us/201210/unconditional-positive-regard (accessed November 26, 2014)

6   Worldview is defined by the German concept *Weltanschauung*, which denotes one's view of world and being and is related to how one sees personality in terms of self-transformation cf. http://www.theneworder.org/national-socialism/idea-movement/weltanschauung/ (accessed September 30, 2014); Berger, Peter, An Invitation to Sociology: A Humanistic Perspective. New York, Doubleday and Company, Inc., 1963.

7   Self-transformation and self-actualization in the self-study refer to healing, that is bringing all that is unbalanced into balance and proportion. Engendering in the human personality the synthesizing of all parts that are dysfunctional elements thereby engendering functionality of the organic human personality and being cf. Holistic/Holism, http://www.webmd.com/balance/guide/what-is-holistic-medicine. (accessed September 30, 2014). Self-actualization is the becoming of the personality into a state of healing, self-transformation and creative maturity. This is the transformation of the person synthesizing both being and metabeing and values with meta-values; cf. Self-Actualization, http://psychology.about.com/od/theoriesofpersonality/a/hierarchyneeds_2.htm (accessed September 30, 2014).

8   Cultural Identity, http://en.wikipedia.org/wiki/Cultural_identity (accessed December 05, 2014) cf. Theories Linking Culture and Psychology, http://www.bridgingworlds.org/pdfs/1processes.pdf (accessed December 05, 2014)

9   Shadow in Jungian psychology refers to the aspect of the unconscious that is irrational. Shadow is often negative in connotation but can be somewhat positive. It is reflective of the father archetype in the symbolic thinking of Carl Jung: http://en.wikipedia.org/wiki/Shadow_(psychology) (accessed December 03, 2014); Shadow self, http://jungian.org/page3.html (December 03, 2014)

Notes

10 Cherokee Mythology, http://en.wikipedia.org/wiki/Cherokee_mythology, (accessed November 28, 2014); Religion According to Chief Jahtohi Rogers: A People in Exodus, http://cherokeenationofsequoyah.com/greatspirit.html (November 28, 2014)

11 *Terminus* denotes the end of a line or road, in this case, the finality of creation. In the sense of Irenaeus of Lyons, finality is the summing up of all things in Christ, who transfigures the present creation with the newness of glory and resurrection cf. Recapitulation Theory of Atonement, http://www.theopedia.com/Recapitulation_theory_of_atonement (accessed December 05, 2014)

12 Consider the Speck and the Beam, Matthew 7:2-4, http://biblehub.com/matthew/7-3.htm (accessed November 28, 2014)

13 Mindfulness and Vigilance: These two concepts are strongly related. In the New Testament Greek and Eastern Orthodox sense, Vigilance (*nepsis*) from 1 Peter 5:8 calls for continually maintaining a sober heart and mind while watching for thoughts, passions and circumstances that prevent the soul from receiving the mind and wisdom of God in all virtue and fruit of the Spirit. From Zen and Taoism Mindfulness as with Nepsis indicates the ever presence of the soul with self and being. Self-management and virtue occur through ever presence with the flow of moments in self and context. In seeing the flow of thoughts and emotions nonjudgmentally, one true develops discernment of what is wise and heavenly cf. Nepsis, http://en.wikipedia.org/wiki/Nepsis (accessed December 06, 2014); Mindfulness, http://www.psychologytoday.com/basics/mindfulness (accessed December 06, 2014);

Mindfulness (psychology), http://en.wikipedia.org/wiki/Mindfulness_(psychology) (accessed December 06, 2014)

Chapter Two

14 Contextual Therapy, http://behavenet.com/contextual-therapy (November 28, 2014); Contextual Therapy, http://therapycenters.com/2012/09/contextual-therapy/

(November 28, 2014)

15 Slavery in America, http://www.history.com/topics/black-history/slavery (accessed December 07, 2014)

16 African-American Spirituals, http://www.authentichistory.com/1600-1859/3-spirituals/index.html (December 07, 2014)

17 Slavery and the Churches, http://www.christianchronicler.com/history1/slavery_and_the_churches.htm (accessed December 07, 2014); Let My People Go: The Catholic Church and Slavery, http://www.catholiceducation.org/en/controversy/common-misconceptions/let-my-people-go-the-catholic-church-and-slavery.html (accessed December 07, 2014).

18 Ebonics,http://en.wikipedia.org/wiki/Ebonics_(word) (accessed November 29, 2014)

19 Calvinism, http://www.britannica.com/EBchecked/topic/90293/Calvinism (accessed December 07, 2014); America: Experiment or Destiny, http://www.americanheritage.com/content/america-experiment-or-destiny (accessed December 07, 2014); Book Review, http://www.christreformedbaptist.org/uploads/1/0/6/4/10645670/book_review.baptist_roots_in_america.pdf (accessed December 07, 2014); Puritan, http://en.wikipedia.org/

Notes

wiki/Puritan (accessed December 07, 2014); Manifest Destiny, http://www.u-s-history.com/pages/h337.html (accessed December 07, 2014); John Calvin and the Shaping of America, http://open.salon.com/blog/susanthur/2009/07/10/john_calvin_and_the_shaping_of_america (accessed December 07, 2014)

20 Black people, http://en.wikipedia.org/wiki/Black_people (accessed December 07, 2014)

Chapter Three

21 Acculturation, http://en.wikipedia.org/wiki/Acculturation cf. Fitzgerald, Thomas K: *Metaphors of Identity.* Albany: State University of New York Press, 1993.

22 Acculturation and Assimilation, http://www.differencebetween.com/difference-between-acculturation-and-vs-assimilation/ (accessed September 30, 2014) cf. Op. cit

23 Cultural Change and Adaptation, http://www.britannica.com/EBchecked/topic/27505/anthropology/236838/Cultural-change-and-adaptation (accessed September 30, 2014); Cultural Adaptation, http://oregonstate.edu/instruct/anth370/gloss.html (accessed September 30, 2014); Psychological Adaptation, http://psychologydictionary.org/adaptation/ (accessed September 30, 2014); Evolutionary Adaptation, http://www.nas.edu/evolution/Definitions.html (accessed September 30, 2014) cf. Op. cit.; Mesoudi, Alex: *Cultural Evolution: How Darwinian Theory Can Explain Human Culture and Synthesize the Social Sciences.* Chicago: The University of Chicago Press, 2011.

24 Re've'sz, G., *Introduction to The Psychology of Music.* Norman, Oklahoma: University of Oklahoma Press, 1954,

pp. 236f., 243.

25 Op. cit. p. 243.

26 Op. cit.

27 Introduction to the Elements of Design: Point, http://char.txa.cornell.edu/language/element/element.htm (accessed August 28, 2013); Element, http://char.txa.cornell.edu/language/element/element.htm (accessed August 28, 2013); John Lovett, Elements and Principles of Design http://www.johnlovett.com/test.htm (accessed August 28, 2013);

28 The Elements of Expository Writing, http://www.grossmont.edu/marilyn.ivanovici/WritingGuides/0-ELEMENTS.nolines.PDF (accessed August 29, 2013); The Basic Elements of Poetry, http://lifestyle.iloveindia.com/lounge/basic-elements-of-poetry-4793.html; The Elements of Poetry, http://bcs.bedfordstmartins.com/virtualit/poetry/elements.html (accessed August 29, 2013).

29 Re've'sz, G: *Introduction to The Psychology of Music*. Norman, Oklahoma: University of Oklahoma Press, 1954, 244.

30 Brunner, Jerome: *The Process of Education*. Cambridge: Harvard University Press, 1960, pp. 56-59.

31 Levine, Ann: *Understanding Psychology*. New York: Random House, Inc., 1977, p. 111.

32 Similarity, http://en.wikipedia.org/wiki/Similarity_(geometry) (accessed December 09, 2014)

33 Continuity, http://www.merriam-webster.com/dictionary/continuity (accessed December 09, 2014)

34 Gestalt, http://www.merriam-webster.com/dictionary/gestalt (accessed December 09, 2014)

Notes

35 Levine, Ann: *Understanding Psychology*. New York: Random House, Inc., 1977, p. 111.

36 Brubaker, Dale L., Curriculum Planning: They Dynamics of Theory and Practice, Dallas, Texas: Scott, Foresman and Company, 1982 cf. Berger, Peter L., Op. cit.

37 Op. cit., p. 112.

38 Sufficit(s): This is my terminology to describe the opposite of a deficit in the human personality. Consequently, strengths and positive personality traits are sufficits while deficits refer to needs and weaknesses in personality trait make-up.

39 Carl Rogers, http://www.simplypsychology.org/carl-rogers.html (accessed December 09, 2014)

40 Self-actualization, http://en.wikipedia.org/wiki/Self-actualization; Individuation, http://www.amazon.com/Becoming-Introduction-Jungs-Concept-Individuation/dp/1926715594; http://en.wikipedia.org/wiki/Carl_Jung

41 *Pedagogos,* http://www.wordcentral.com/cgi-bin/student?pedagogue;http://www.jstor.org/

42 Culture, http://www.tamu.edu/faculty/choudhury/culture.html , (accessed September 05, 2013).

43 Culture and Harmony definition google search.

44 Unity, http://arthistory.about.com/cs/glossaries/g/u_unity.htm (accessed September 05, 2013).

45 Structure, http://www.google.com/#q=Structure+definition&safe=off , (accessed September 05, 2013).

46 Texture, The Free Dictionary by Farflex, http://www.thefreedictionary.com/texture, (accessed September 05, 2013).

47 A Short History of Tonantzin…, http://yeoldeconsciousnessshoppe.com/art261.html (accessed December 09, 2014)

48 Kimberly Wallace-Sanders, A Century of Race, Gender, and Southern Memory, http://www.press.umich.edu/pdf/9780472116140-intro.pdf (accessed September 05, 2013).

49 Jennifer Flood Eastin, Impact of Absent Father-Figures on Male Subjects and the Correlation to Juvenile Delinquency: Findings and Implications, http://digital.library.unt.edu/ark:/67531/metadc4332/m2/1/high_res_d/dissertation.pdf (accessed September 05, 2013); Should Juvenile Delinquency by Abolished? https://www.ncjrs.gov/App/publications/abstract.aspx?ID=48016 (accessed September 05, 2013).

50 Love alliteration, Love's labours lost Long-lost love letterLive, laugh, love, http://answers.yahoo.com/question/index?qid=20130206165648AAtuVhE (accessed September 06, 2013)

51 Setting the mood with assonance, http://examples.yourdictionary.com/assonance-examples.htm (accessed September 06, 2013)

52 List of Animal Sounds, http://en.wikipedia.org/wiki/List_of_animal_sounds

Chapter Four

53 Personality traits, http://psychology.about.com/od/profilesal/p/gordon-allport.htm (accessed September

06, 2013). G. W. Allport (1937). *Personality: A Psychological Interpretation.* New York: Holt, Rinehart, & Winston; G.W. Allport (1961). *Pattern and growth in Personality.* New York: Holt, Rinehart, & Winston.

54 16-trait theory, http://psychology.about.com/od/trait-theories-personality/a/16-personality-factors.htm (accessed September 06, 2013); R. B. Cattell (1946). *The Description and Measurement of Personality.* New York, NY: Harcourt, Brace, & World.

55 The three-factor theory, http://psychology.about.com/od/theoriesofpersonality/a/trait-theory.htm (accessed September 06, 2013); H.J. Eysenck (1992). "Four Ways Five Factors Are Not Basic. *Personality and Individual Differences, 13*, 667-673

56 *The Big Five Personality Dimensions,* http://psychology.about.com/od/personalitydevelopment/a/bigfive.htm, (accessed September 07, 2013); What is personality? http://personalityspirituality.net/articles/what-is-personality/ (accessed September 07, 2013).

57 Op. Cit.

58 638 personality traits, http://ideonomy.mit.edu/essays/traits.html (accessed September 07, 2013);

59 Ideonomy, http://ideonomy.mit.edu/intro.html (accessed September 07, 2013).

Chapter Five

60 The three client personality sketches are individual, male client representations reflecting the sample of my client caseload from December 04, 2015 through September 23, 2013. This includes a total of 534 male clients counseled since

I began counseling at Insight Human Services on February 21, 2005. The totality of this this sample is divided by 3. In turn, each subdivision of 178 clients represent the cultural group of this study, namely, African-American, Anglo-American Caucasian and Hispanic American.

Chapter Six

61 Person-centered approach, http://www.bapca.org.uk/about/what-is-it.html (accessed September 14, 2013); How to Apply Person Centered Therapy Techniques to Your Life, Without Paying for Therapy, http://voices.yahoo.com/how-apply-person-centered-therapy-techniques-to-6714294.html?cat=72n (accessed September 14, 2013).

62 Unconditional Positive Regard with Genuineness, http://www.psychologytoday.com/blog/what-doesnt-kill-us/201210/unconditional-positive-regard (accessed November 26, 2014)

63 Suzuki Method, wikipedia.org/wiki/Suzuki_method (accessed December 12, 2014)

64 Mindfulness, Mindfulness (psychology), http://en.wikipedia.org/wiki/Mindfulness_(psychology) (accessed December 06, 2014).

65 Nepsis, http://en.wikipedia.org/wiki/Nepsis (accessed December 06, 2014)

66 Mitzvah, http://en.wikipedia.org/wiki/Mitzvah (December 12, 2014)

Chapter Seven

67 Derya Gungor, Immigration and Acculturation

Notes

in Adolescence, http://www.child-encyclopedia.com/documents/GungorANGxp1.pdf (accessed September 19, 2013).

Chapter Eight

68 *Therapeuo* denotes in New Testament Greek lexical studies as indicating service, ministry and healing. In ancient Hellenic culture, a healing order among Jews in Alexandria, Egypt demonstrated ministers of healing called the *Therapeutae*. http://www.bibletools.org/index.cfm/fuseaction/Lexicon.show/ID/G2323/therapeuo.htm; http://en.wikipedia.org/wiki/Therapeutae

Bibliography

A Short History of Tonantzin…, http://yeoldeconsciousnessshoppe.com/art261.html (accessed December 09, 2014)

Acculturation, http://en.wikipedia.org/wiki/Acculturation (accessed September 30, 2014).

Acculturation and Assimilation, http://www.differencebetween.com/difference-between-acculturation-and-vs-assimilation/ (accessed September 30, 2014).

African-American Spirituals, http://www.authentichistory.com/1600-1859/3-spirituals/index.html (December 07, 2014).

Allport, G. W. *Personality: A Psychological Interpretation.* New York: Holt, Rinehart, & Winston, 1937.

Allport, G.W. *Pattern and growth in Personality.* New York: Holt, Rinehart, & Winston. 1967.

Ahmed, Shamshad et al., *What Does It Mean to Be a Culturally Competent Counselor? The Special Issue on Multicultural Social Justice Leadership Development,* Guest Editor: Carlos P. Zalaquett, University of South Florida; http://www.psysr.org/jsacp/ahmed-v3n1-11_17-28.pdf (accessed September 30, 2014).

Bibliography

America: Experiment or Destiny, http://www.americanheritage.com/content/america-experiment-or-destiny (accessed December 07, 2014).

Berger, Peter L., An Invitation to Sociology: A Humanistic Perspective. New York, Doubleday and Company, Inc., 1963.

Book Review, http://www.christreformedbaptist.org/uploads/1/0/6/4/10645670/book_review.baptist_roots_in_america.pdf (accessed December 07, 2014).

Brubaker, Dale L., Curriculum Planning: They Dynamics of Theory and Practice, Dallas, Texas: Scott, Foresman and Company, 1982.

Brunner, Jerome: *The Process of Education*. Cambridge: Harvard University Press, 1960, pp. 56-59.

Cattell, R. B. *The Description and Measurement of Personality*. New York, NY: Harcourt,. Brace, & World, 1946.

Calvinism, http://www.britannica.com/EBchecked/topic/90293/Calvinism (accessed December 07, 2014).

Carl Rogers, http://www.simplypsychology.org/carl-rogers.html (accessed December 09, 2014)

Cherokee Mythology, http://en.wikipedia.org/wiki/Cherokee_mythology, (accessed November 28, 2014); Religion According to Chief Jahtohi Rogers: A People in Exodus, http://cherokeenationofsequoyah.com/greatspirit.html (November 28, 2014)

Consider the Beam and the Speck, Matthew 7:2-4, http://biblehub.com/matthew/7-3.htm (accessed November 28, 2014).

Contextual Therapy, Contextual Therapy, http://behavenet.com/contextual-therapy (November 28, 2014);

Contextual Therapy, http://therapycenters.com/2012/09/contextual-therapy/ (November 28, 2014)

Continuity, http://www.merriam-webster.com/dictionary/continuity (accessed December 09, 2014)

Conus, Leon and Olga, http://www.amazon.com/Fundamentals-Piano-Technique-Olga-Conus/product-reviews/0874876605 (accessed on September 30, 2014);

Conus, Olga, http://homepages.uwp.edu/mckeever/MadameConusArticle.html (accessed on September 30, 2014).

Counselling and Self-awareness, http://www.thecounsellorsguide.co.uk/counselling-self-awareness.html (accessed September 21, 2013);

Culture, http://www.tamu.edu/faculty/choudhury/culture.html, (accessed September 05, 2013).

Cultural Adaptation, http://oregonstate.edu/instruct/anth370/gloss.html (accessed September 30, 2014).

Cultural Change and Adaptation, http://www.britannica.com/EBchecked/topic/27505/anthropology/236838/Cultural-change-and-adaptation (accessed September 30, 2014).

Cultural Identity, http://en.wikipedia.org/wiki/Cultural_identity (accessed December 05,

Bibliography

Ebonics, http://en.wikipedia.org/wiki/Ebonics_(word) (accessed November 29, 2014)

Element, http://char.txa.cornell.edu/language/element/element.htm (accessed August 28, 2013).

Eysenck, H. J. "Four Ways Five Factors Are Not Basic. *Personality and Individual Differences, 13*, 667-673, 1992.

Evolutionary Adaptation, http://www.nas.edu/evolution/Definitions.html (accessed September 30, 2014).

Fitzgerald, Thomas K: *Metaphors of Identity.* Albany: State University of New York Press, 1993.

Flood Eastin, Jennifer. *Impact of Absent Father Figures on Male Subjects and the Correlation to Juvenile Delinquency: Findings and Implications,* http://digital.library.unt.edu/ark:/67531/metadc4332/m2/1/high_res_d/dissertation.pdf (accessed September 05, 2013).

Gestalt, http://www.merriam-webster.com/dictionary/gestalt (accessed December 09, 2014)

Gungor, Derya. *Immigration and Acculturation in Adolescence,* http://www.child-encyclopedia.com/documents/GungorANGxp1.pdf (accessed September 30, 2014).

Holistic/Holism, http://www.webmd.com/balance/guide/what-is-holistic-medicine. (accessed September 30, 2014).

How to Apply Person Centered Therapy Techniques to Your Life, Without Paying for Therapy, http://voices.yahoo.com/how-apply-person-centered-therapy-techniques-to-6714294.html?cat=72n (accessed September 14, 2013)

Ideonomy, http://ideonomy.mit.edu/intro.html (accessed September 07, 2013).

Individuation, http://www.amazon.com/Becoming-Introduction-Jungs-Concept-Individuation/dp/1926715594 (accessed September 30, 2014).

Individuation, http://en.wikipedia.org/wiki/Carl_Jung (accessed September 30, 2014).

Introduction to the Elements of Design: Point, http://char.txa.cornell.edu/language/element/element.htm, **(accessed August 28, 2013).**

John Calvin and the Shaping of America, http://open.salon.com/blog/susanthur/2009/07/10/john_calvin_and_the_shaping_of_america (accessed December 07, 2014).

Katalambano, http://biblehub.com/greek/2638.htm (accessed December 02, 2014).

Kfeir, http://kfeir.com (accessed November 25, 2014).

Kfeir, http://www.kfeir.com/village.html (accessed November 25, 2014).

Kfeir, http://en.wikipedia.org/wiki/Kfeir (accessed November 25, 2014).

Let My People Go: The Catholic Church and Slavery, http://www.catholiceducation.org/en/controversy/common-misconceptions/let-my-people-go-the-catholic-church-and-

Bibliography

slavery.html (accessed December 07, 2014).

Levine, Ann: *Understanding Psychology*. New York: Random House, Inc., 1977.

List of Animal Sounds, http://en.wikipedia.org/wiki/List_of_animal_sounds (accessed October 2, 2014).

Love Alliteration, Love's labours lostLong-lost love letterLive, laugh, love, http://answers.yahoo.com/question/index?qid=20130206165648AAtuVhE (accessed September 06, 2013).

Lovett, John. *Elements and Principles of Design* http://www.johnlovett.com/test.htm (accessed August 28, 2013).

Mesoudi, Alex: *Cultural Evolution: How Darwinian Theory Can Explain Human Culture and Synthesize the Social Sciences.* Chicago: The University of Chicago Press, 2011.

Mindfulness, http://www.psychologytoday.com/basics/mindfulness (accessed December 06, 2014);

Mindfulness (psychology), http://en.wikipedia.org/wiki/Mindfulness_(psychology) (accessed December 06, 2014).

Mitzvah, http://en.wikipedia.org/wiki/Mitzvah (December 12, 2014).

Nepsis, http://en.wikipedia.org/wiki/Nepsis (accessed December 06, 2014).

Pedagogos, http://www.wordcentral.com/cgi-bin/student?pedagogue (accessed September 30, 2014)

Person-centered approach, http://www.bapca.org.uk/about/what-is-it.html **(accessed September 14, 2013).**

Personality traits, http://psychology.about.com/od/profilesal/p/gordon-allport.htm (accessed September 06, 2013).

[638] Personality Traits, http://ideonomy.mit.edu/essays/traits.html (accessed September 07, 2013).

Proportion, http://dictionary.reference.com/browse/proportion (accessed December 09, 2014).

Psychological Adaptation, http://psychologydictionary.org/adaptation/ (accessed September 30, 2014).

Puritan, http://en.wikipedia.org/wiki/Puritan (accessed December 07, 2014); Manifest Destiny, http://www.u-s-history.com/pages/h337.html (accessed December 07, 2014).

Re've'sz, G: *Introduction to The Psychology of Music.* Norman, Oklahoma: University of Oklahoma Press, 1954.

Recapitulation Theory of Atonement, http://www.theopedia.com/Recapitulation_theory_of_atonement (accessed December 05, 2014)

Self-Actualization, http://en.wikipedia.org/wiki/Self-actualization (accessed September 30, 2014).

Setting the mood with assonance, http://examples.yourdictionary.com/assonance-examples.htm (accessed September 06, 2013).

Shadow (psychology), http://en.wikipedia.org/wiki/Shadow_(psychology) (accessed December 03, 2014).

Shadow self, http://jungian.org/page3.html (December 03, 2014).

Bibliography

Should Juvenile Delinquency by Abolished? https://www.ncjrs.gov/App/publications/abstract.aspx?ID=48016 (accessed September 05, 2013).

Similarity, http://en.wikipedia.org/wiki/Similarity_(geometry) (accessed December 09, 2014)

Slavery and the Churches, http://www.christianchronicler.com/history1/slavery_and_the_churches.htm (accessed December 07, 2014).

Structure, http://www.google.com/#q=Structure+definition&safe=off, (accessed September 05, 2013).

Suzuki Method, wikipedia.org/wiki/Suzuki_method (accessed December 12, 2014)

Texture, The Free Dictionary by Farflex, http://www.thefreedictionary.com/texture, (accessed September 05, 2013).

Therapeutae, http://www.bibletools.org/index.cfm/fuseaction/Lexicon.show/ID/G2323/therapeuo.htm; http://en.wikipedia.org/wiki/Therapeutae (accessed September 30, 2014).

The Basic Elements of Poetry, http://lifestyle.iloveindia.com/lounge/basic-elements-of-poetry-4793.html (accessed August 29, 2013).

The Big Five Personality Dimensions, http://psychology.about.com/od/personalitydevelopment/a/bigfive.htm, (accessed September 07, 2013).

The Elements of Expository Writing, http://www.grossmont.edu/marilyn.ivanovici/WritingGuides/0-ELEMENTS.nolines.PDF (accessed August 29, 2013

The Elements of Poetry, http://bcs.bedfordstmartins.com/virtualit/poetry/elements.html (accessed August 29, 2013).

The Three-Factor theory, http://psychology.about.com/od/theoriesofpersonality/a/trait-theory.htm (accessed September 06, 2013);

Theories Linking Culture and Psychology, http://www.bridgingworlds.org/pdfs/1processes.pdf (accessed December 05, 2014).

[16-]Trait Theory, http://psychology.about.com/od/trait-theories-personality/a/16-personality-factors.htm (accessed September 06, 2013);

Unconditional Positive Regard with Genuineness, http://www.psychologytoday.com/blog/what-doesnt-kill-us/201210/unconditional-positive-regard (accessed November 26, 2014)

Unity, http://arthistory.about.com/cs/glossaries/g/u_unity.htm (accessed September 05, 2013).

Wallace-Sanders, Kimberly. *A Century of Race, Gender, and Southern Memory*, http://www.press.umich.edu/pdf/9780472116140-intro.pdf (accessed September 05, 2013).

Weltanschauung, . http://www.theneworder.org/national-socialism/idea-movement/weltanschauung/ (accessed September 30, 2014).

What is personality? http://personalityspirituality.net/articles/what-is-personality/ (accessed September 07, 2013).

Index

A

acculturation 19, 29, 31, 33, 39, 114, 115, 116, 117, 118, 120, 125, 126, 135, 141, 142

Acculturation 135

African-American 9, 13, 14, 15, 16, 18, 30, 31, 32, 34, 35, 36, 58, 59, 72, 77, 90, 91, 94, 109, 114, 118, 125, 134, 142

agreeable 66, 75, 79, 85

allegory 60

alliteration 61, 138, 147

Allport 65, 69, 138, 139, 142, 148

Anglo-American 31, 32, 33, 34, 35, 36, 39, 59

apprehend 4, 42, 44, 131

apprehension 4, 41, 44

artistic 1, 3, 10, 39, 40, 62, 67, 89, 106, 127

assimilation 33, 39, 125, 126, 135, 142

Assimilation 142

Aztec 29, 36, 58

151

B

balance [40—41—42—43—44—47—51—53—54—56]

beauty [6—10—12—26—40—41—44—50—98]

belongingness [17—49—86—90—91—92—94—100—108—113—117]

binary opposites [40—68]

C

Calvinism [35—134—143]

Calvinistic [35—59]

categories [42—46—53—54—66—68—69]

category [68]

Cattell, Raymond [65]

City on the Hill [36]

closed [66—67—76—85—91—120]

cognitive behavior [17]

collaboration [95]

color [34—42—54—55—56—67—69—99—107—111—113—126]

comparison [32—43—54—55—113—114—120]

composition [40—43—44—45—47—48—54—56—57—68—69—96—97—98—103—106—107—109—110]

Index

111___112___113___118___119___120___125___128

comprehend ⁴—⁴¹

comprehending ⁴

connotation ¹³²

Connotation ⁶²

conscientious ⁶⁶___⁶⁷___⁷⁵___⁷⁹___⁸⁴

consciousness ¹⁸___¹⁹___⁴⁷___⁴⁸___¹³⁸___¹⁴²

content ¹²⁴—¹³⁴

context ¹³³___¹³⁴___¹⁴⁴

contextual therapy ²⁸

Contextual Therapy ¹³⁴—¹⁴⁴

continuity ⁴⁰___⁴³___⁴⁶___⁴⁷___¹³⁶

contrast ¹⁶___³⁰___³²___⁴²___⁴³___⁵³___⁵⁵___⁵⁷___⁶²

Contrast ⁵⁴

counseling ᵛ___1___3___6___7___8___9___11___12___13___17___19___21___22___25___27___30___32___36___40___41___42___45___46___48___49___50___51___52___58___59___60___62___71___72___76___77___83___84___86___89___91___92___93___94___95___96___99___100___101___102___103___105___106___108___109___110___112___113___114___117___118___120___123___124___125___127___128___140___158

create ¹²___¹⁷___⁴²___⁴⁴___⁴⁷___⁴⁹___⁵³___⁵⁴___⁵⁵___⁵⁷___⁶⁷___⁸⁷___⁹⁰___⁹⁸___¹⁰²___¹⁰³___¹⁰⁸___¹¹⁰___¹¹³

153

creativity 6—80—99—102—103—107

cultural diversity 8—9—127

cultural identity 31—33—132—144

culture 18—28—31—33—34—35—39—49—51—52—53—56—57—58—59—61

Culture 53

culture and ethnicity 49—52

D

deficits 39—40—49—51—54—57—62

denotation 62

design 40—41—42—44—48—52—55

development 47—51—55—57—61—94—96—99—113—120—128

developmental 47—61—78

dynamic 42—43—54—55—124—137—143

dysfunctional 13—132

E

Eastern Orthodox 5—7—8—10—20—22—24—133

Ebonics 35—134—145

ego 18

Index

elements 24, 40, 41, 42, 43, 47, 48, 49, 56, 57, 62, 69, 71, 103, 109, 132, 136, 149, 150

empowering 22, 77, 112

equilibrium 42

esthetic 40, 42, 43, 44, 47, 48

ethnicity 13, 15, 36, 49, 52, 53, 109

Eysenk, Hans 65

extroversion 66, 67, 68, 75

F

Fiske, Donald 65, 66, 68, 69

fragmentation 22, 29, 40, 54, 62, 76, 113

G

gestalt 47, 71, 136, 145

goal 55, 92, 97, 105, 127

goal oriented 55

goals 55, 92, 95, 96, 97, 105, 127

guide 40, 52, 101, 111, 124, 127, 132, 145

guiding 36, 89, 97, 99, 105, 111, 118

H

harmony 25—42—43—53—54—55—56—65—66—69—77—80—86—103—105—106—107—111—118—119

Hebrew 5—6

Hispanic 13—14—15—16—18—28—29—31—32—33—34—35—36—58—59—71—72—81—90—92—94—114—115—116—119—125—140

Hostile 66—75—79—85

I

identity 4

Incan 36

individuation 6—20—50—125—152

intellect 5—44

inter-reflective 5

interrelationship 3

introversion 66—67—68—76—85—86—105—106—107—108

intuitive 44—45

J

Jesus 5—6—25—101

Jung 6—50—132—137—146—152

Index

Jung's individuation [6]

K

knowledge [19, 29, 31, 36, 41, 45, 46, 47, 48, 49, 53, 89, 90, 96, 99]

L

language [11, 18, 19, 20, 33, 34, 35, 36, 40, 52, 53, 57, 58, 60, 62, 67, 74, 103, 126, 136, 145, 146]

life [3, 5, 6, 17, 18, 21, 22, 23, 25, 40, 47, 49, 51, 54, 55, 60, 62, 85, 92, 94, 96, 97, 99, 102, 105, 106, 107, 108, 109, 111, 112, 114, 115, 124, 125, 158]

Likert scale [68, 94, 120]

listen [51, 58, 59, 62, 90, 95, 96, 117, 120]

listening [4, 10, 42, 49, 51, 60, 61, 90, 91, 92, 94, 96, 97, 98, 108]

M

Madame and Leon Conus. [52]

Martin Luther King [30, 58]

Maslow [6, 50, 152]

meaning [12, 28, 51, 60, 68, 108, 112, 113, 120, 131]

mentor [1, 52, 71, 89, 97, 158]

mentoring ⁶²—¹²⁴

metaphor ²¹—²³—³³—⁴⁰—⁵⁸—¹¹⁰—¹²⁸

Mexican ²⁹—⁵⁸

mind ⁴—⁵—⁶—²⁵—⁴⁴—⁵²—¹⁰¹—¹⁰²—¹⁰³—¹⁰⁸—¹³³

monotony ⁴³—⁵⁵

motivation ²⁵—⁵⁵—¹¹⁰

music ⁷—¹⁰—¹¹—²⁰—²¹—²²—²⁹—⁴²—⁴³—⁴⁵—⁴⁶—⁴⁷—⁴⁸—⁵³—⁵⁴—⁵⁵—⁵⁶—⁶⁹—⁷³—⁹⁴—⁹⁷—⁹⁸—¹⁰⁵—¹⁰⁶—¹⁰⁷—¹⁰⁹—¹⁵⁸—¹⁵⁹

N

Neurotic ⁶⁶—⁶⁷—⁷⁵—⁷⁹—⁸⁵

O

Onomatopoeia ⁶¹

Ontological ⱽⁱ—³—¹⁵²

Ontology ⁱᵛ

Open ⁶⁶—⁷⁵—⁷⁹—⁸⁴—⁹¹

openness ⁶⁶—⁶⁷—⁷⁶—⁸⁰—⁸¹—⁸⁵—⁸⁶—⁹²—⁹⁵—¹¹⁸

openness and collaboration ⁹⁵

opposites ⁴⁰—⁵³—⁵⁴—⁵⁵—⁶⁸—¹³⁷

P

Index

paradigm [1—40—53—101]

parent [13—14—62—83—93—94]

Parental Involvement [93]

Pattern [139—142]

patterns [46—47—56]

pedagogue [51—52—124—125—137—147]

persona [4—87—98]

personality [1—3—4—6—7—8—15—18—19—20—22—23—25—36—39—40—41—44—45—46—47—49—50—51—52—53—54—55—57—58—59—62—65—66—67—68—69—71—72—76—77—80—86—90—92—93—96—98—99—103—105—106—107—108—109—110—113—114—118—119—120—123—124—125—127—128—132—137—139—150—158]

personal symbols [51]

person-centeredness [89]

phenomenological [41]

piano students [50—51—95—96—97]

poetry [11—41—42—55—56—69—136—149—150]

population [36—39—71—72—123—158]

portrait [113—125—127—128]

portraiture [12—113—124]

proportion 6—40—41—43—44—47—53—69—132—148

Protestant 7—8—29—35—73—91—100

Protestant Evangelical 35

Protestantism 20—35

psyche 3—4—5—6—47—49—52—102—103—124

psychodynamics 7

Q

quality 50—54—99

R

rhythm 42—56—98—106

Rogers, Carl 6—49—137—143

Roman Catholic 10—30—35

S

seat of mind 5

self iv—1—3—4—5—6—8—12—14—17—18—19—20—25—36—39—42—45—46—47—49—50—51—60—76—78—80—81—86—87—89—90—97—98—100—101—102—103—105—108—109—110—111—112—113—114—115—116—118—119—124—125—127—128—131—132—133—144—148—152

self-actualization 1—6—17—20—50—98—108—124—125—132—152

Index

self-awareness 3—4—25—127—128—131—144

self-reflection 3—25—98—101—127—128

Similarity 136—149

Socrates 5—6

sontaneous 66—75—79—84

sound 43—54—61

spiritual 13—18—22—44—48—65—100—101—103—124—125—127

spirituality 6—29—53—99—100—101—102—127

Spontaneous 66—75—79—84

stable 66—75—79—85

stagnancy 55

story 19—23—49—92—93—94—96—97—98

stream of consciousness 47

structural 57

structure 18—41—42—45—55—56—57—97—109

sufficits 40—49—51—54—62—68—92—93—95—99—109—137

symbolic 58

symbols 18—51—58—59—60

symmetry 40—42—43—69—86—98—103

synergistic 6

synergize 4—46—89

synergy 5

T

tactful questioning 91

teachability 99

teaching 6—7—9—10—11—12—25—30—32—51—52—95—106—109—111—118—124

telos 6—95—96—97—98

terminus 24—50—102

Therapeutic 49

therapist v—27—32—89—90—93—94—95—96—98—108—110—115—116—123—125

therapy 9—13—17—21—28—40—50—52—61—72—73—77—89—94—96—98—114—134—140—144—146

tone 50—51—54—60—61—69—77—81—86—98—99—106—107

trait 69—76—77—80—81—85—86—137—139—150

traits 18—29—33—34—40—41—45—50—51—52—53—54—55—56—57—59—65—66—67—68—69—71—76—80—81—85—86—90—93—96—108—110—116—119—123—125—127—137—138—139—148—158

transform 1

transformation 6—24—25—108—127—132

transforming 6—112

U

unconditional positive regard 17—49—90—100

unity 4—6—25—41—42—43—44—56—57—69—86—103—115—137—150

V

value 19—20—24—36—42—44—113—127—158

W

Weltanschauung 132—150

whole 4—6—12—17—25—40—43—46—50—51—52—54—55—56—57—96—97

whole being 4—52

wholeness 1—6—12—17—20—26—39—40—41—42—44—62—69

Wisdom 4

worldview 19—20—21—22—25—47—49—53—71—77—98—99—105—107—108—110—111—112—113—118—119

writing 8—17—41—42—46—54—55—56—57—58—59—61—69—115—123—158

Index

Index

About the Author

As a counseling professional, the author has experienced the value and power of autobiography writing. He has continued to grow and mature in it as a musician, writer and counselor. Through his education and struggles in everyday life, he has continued to grow in the traits of is life that have shaped his personality as a counselor, mentor, artist. The road to professional counseling grew out of his education experience as a teacher, musician, minister, and priest. The author works with the student age population growing out of his educational background and licensure as a teacher of grades K-12, but specializing with grades 9-12 and later those of college age. His emphasis of study began in junior high school with the study of music and later becoming a piano major in college.

Colophon
Tites in Gabriola
Text in Baskerville
Book set in Adobe Indesign CC

Gabriola is a display typeface designed by John Hudson. Named after Gabriola Island, in British Columbia, Canada, it is primarily intended for use at larger sizes, but can also work well in short passages of text. The Gabriola font can add elegance and grace to titles, subheads and other situations in which a more decorative style of type is appropriate.

The design of Gabriola was inspired by an idea from music: that the same melody can be played in multiple modes, each with its own expressive characteristics. Gabriola was developed with advanced OpenType features and has been optimized for advanced ClearType rendering to improve legibility on screen.

Baskerville is a transitional serif typeface designed in 1757 by John Baskerville (1706–1775) in Birmingham, England. Baskerville is classified as a transitional typeface, positioned between the old style typefaces of William Caslon, and the newer styles of Giambattista Bodoni & Firmin Didot.

www.ingramcontent.com/pod-product-compliance
Lightning Source LLC
Chambersburg PA
CBHW051102160426
43193CB00010B/1286